Library of Pastoral Care

THE PASTORAL CARE OF
THE MENTALLY ILL

The Library of Pastoral Care

TITLES ALREADY PUBLISHED

Principles of Pastoral Counselling
R. S. Lee

Casework and Pastoral Care
Jean Heywood

Marriage Preparation
Martin Parsons

Marriage Counselling
Kenneth Preston

Sick Call: A Book on the Pastoral Care of the Physically Ill
Kenneth Child

Pastoral Care in Hospitals
Norman Autton

Pastoral Care of the Mentally Ill
Norman Autton

Caring for the Elderly
H. P. Steer

The Pastoral Care of the Dying
Norman Autton

The Pastoral Care of the Bereaved
Norman Autton

IN PREPARATION

The Pastoral Care of Children
Anthony Denney

Understanding the Adolescent
Michael Hare Duke

Retreats
W. R. Derry (editor)

In his own Parish: Pastoral Care in Parochial Visiting
Kenneth Child

Hearing Confessions
Kenneth N. Ross

Other volumes are planned

The
Pastoral Care of the
Mentally Ill

NORMAN AUTTON

Director of Training
Church Assembly Hospital Chaplaincies Council

LONDON
S·P·C·K
1969

First published in 1963
by S.P.C.K.
Holy Trinity Church
Marylebone Road
London N.W.1

Second edition, revised and reset, 1969

Made and printed in Great Britain by
William Clowes and Sons, Limited
London and Beccles

SBN 281 00872 8

DEDICATED TO
FATHER, MICHAEL, AND MARY
—MY FAMILY—
WHOSE CO-OPERATION
MADE POSSIBLE
THIS PUBLICATION

Contents

Acknowledgements

Thanks are due to the following for permission to quote extracts from copyright sources:

Abingdon Press, *Understanding and Counselling the Alcoholic* by Howard J. Clinebell, Jr.; The Advisory Committee on Clinical Pastoral Education, "The Theology of Pastoral Care", an address by Paul Tillich in *Clinical Education for the Pastoral Ministry: Proceedings of the Fifth National Conference on Clinical Pastoral Education*; George Allen & Unwin Ltd., *Pastoral Psychology* by G. Bergsten; British Medical Association, Section III of *Divine Healing and Co-operation between Doctors and Clergy*; Burns & Oates Ltd., *Cure of Mind and Cure of Soul* by J. Goldbrunner; *Catholic Digest*, "Psychiatry and Faith" by Karl Stern; Churches' Council of Healing, *A Prescription for Health* by R. W. Luxton; Church Information Office, *The Church's Ministry of Healing— The Report of the Archbishops' Commission 1958*; Constable & Co. Ltd. and The Macmillan Company, *The Individual and his Religion* by Gordon Allport; The Harvill Press Ltd., *Soul and Psyche* by Victor White; Hodder & Stoughton Ltd., *New Concepts of Healing* by A. Graham Ikin; Hodder & Stoughton Ltd. and Rascher & Cie, A. G., Zürich, "Reflections on the Hardships and Inner Stability of the Psychiatrist" by A. Maeder in *Ways to Psychic Health*; Longmans, Green & Co. Ltd. and McGraw-Hill Book Co. Inc., *The Stress of Life* by Hans Selye; McGraw-Hill Book Co., Inc., *Psychiatry and Catholicism* by J. H. Vanderveldt and R. P. Odenwald; The Mercier Press Ltd., *Pastoral Psychology in Practice* by W. Demal; National Association for Mental Health, "Religion and Healing" by Denis Martin in *Mental Health*; The Pastoral Psychology Press, three articles by John C. Ford, C. A. Curran, and Ernest Bruder in *Pastoral Psychology*; Random House, Inc., *Mind and Body* by Flanders Dunbar; Charles Scribner's Sons, *Psychiatry and Mental Health* by James R. Oliver.

Preface

As the original publication of *The Pastoral Care of the Mentally Ill* has been out of print for some time, and much seems to have happened over the years in the whole relationship between the Church and the problems concerning mental illness, it has been felt necessary to revise and abridge the earlier work and include this new edition in the *Library of Pastoral Care*.

The main purpose of the book still remains valid, namely, to provide the priest or minister with relevant information about the various symptoms of mental disorder; to suggest what he can do to meet the needs of the mentally ill and to further his study of the ways in which the good news of the Christian Gospel and all that is best in psychiatry can be so fused as to bring comfort and healing to minds tortured and afflicted by mental disorder.

The word "priest" has been used throughout the text merely as a convenient general term, and it is hoped that it will not be interpreted in any strict or narrow denominational sense.

My gratitude expressed in the first edition both to individual friends who helped in its compilation and the psychiatric hospital where I was formerly chaplain has been deepened over the intervening years. For help in the present revision my sincere thanks are conveyed to my secretary, Mrs Jean Henderson, B.SC.

Michaelmas 1968   NORMAN AUTTON

1

The Church and Mental Illness

... the strained time-ridden faces
Distracted from distraction by distraction
Filled with fancies and empty of meaning
Tumid apathy with no concentration ...

T. S. ELIOT (*Four Quartets*)

I will give you rest.   Matt. 11.28

Mental illness is one of our greatest social problems. In the last hundred years there has been more conquest of pain than in the rest of human history, yet "thirty-two million working days are lost each year through mental and emotional disorders". Nearly half the beds provided by the Health Service are occupied by patients who are mentally ill or handicapped, and mental disorders are the greatest single cause of long-term incapacity. It has also been estimated that one in every four patients consulting their general practitioner is suffering from mental or emotional trouble.

For the vast majority of our people, the strain and stress of modern life distort them into "inferior caricatures of what they might have been" (Harry Stack Sullivan). At no other time in our history has there been so much effort devoted to the study of the sources of love and security. Yet the last half-century has brought an ever-increasing stream of human anxiety and misery. It has been said, not without justification, that psychosis appears to be the stepchild of modern civilization.

Much, however, has been achieved in the past three to four decades, and no longer can Dante's legend—"Abandon hope all ye that enter here"—be seen in all its stark reality engraven on the portals of our hospitals. It is true that architecturally they are still very much out of date, for 65 per cent of them were built before 1891, 42 per cent before 1861, and only four out of the existing 154 psychiatric hospitals were built in the past fifty-three years. The Mental Health Act (1959) introduced a new era in the public attitude towards the care and the treatment of the mentally ill, and it did much to sweep away many of the outmoded legal procedures and terminology affecting those who are ill. (Most of these antediluvian and cumbersome laws were over seventy years old.) The mentally ill can now be treated in exactly the same way (as far as the nature of the disorder allows) and, what is equally important, in exactly the same spirit as the physically ill.

The apparent increase in mental illness can be attributed to many factors: increase in population, greater number of old people, higher rate of senile admissions to psychiatric hospitals, and earlier and more extensive recognition of mental illness. There hangs over our heads, like the sword of Damocles, the threat of atomic warfare, the existence of a cold war, and the danger of guided missiles. The turmoil of the outer world is but a symptom of the disorder that exists within the soul of man. A recent U.N.E.S.C.O. statement pointed out that "since war begins in the minds of men, it is in the minds of men that defence of peace must be constructed".

Jung himself confessed that one-third of the patients who consulted him were suffering from no clinically definable neurosis, but from the emptiness and senselessness of their lives. So many of our people are lonely and isolated, and feel a deep sense of insecurity. With modern travel the world has become a neighbourhood before men have learned to be neighbours.[1] It was André Gide who said that most people

---

[1] "I see them sometimes in church, or in the street, with that harassed look of which you speak, and the urge to help them is strong, sometimes to the point of pain. If they only knew the blessing that God our Lord

are so afraid of finding themselves alone, that they never find themselves at all. The nursery rhyme rings more true than we are apt to realize "I care for nobody, no not I, if nobody cares for me!"

A recent Report on Loneliness, published by the National Council of Social Service, defines loneliness as "the condition of an individual who desires contact with others, but is unable to achieve it". The incidence of loneliness is most heavy, we are told, among the aged, the poor, and the middle income groups—"alive but alone, belonging—where?"[1] More and more instances of neuroses are arising on the vast new housing-estates being erected at the present time. "I was afraid and I hid myself" is a sentiment not confined to the Creation story.

Again we see about us the decay of moral standards, and Karen Horney is of the opinion that "competitiveness and its potential hostilities between fellow beings, fears, diminished self-esteem, result psychologically in the individual feeling that he is isolated".[2]

In this vast problem the Church has an unique part to play, and the need for an informed and positive lead from the Church is imperative. The Church has unrivalled spiritual treasure and resources, for it has the greatest single integrating force to be found in life. The Christian religion, grounded as it is on the redemptive love of God, knowing the vital significance of forgiveness, is the most necessary message for disturbed and anxiety-ridden souls. Hadfield[3] states that he is "convinced that the Christian religion is one of the most

---

was so eager to give them, and how that blessing has in it so much of healing and joy, how swift would they be to reach after it. It is no wonder that the people of the world wear that harried look, for they have nothing to fill the void which is in the human heart. They hunger and thirst, they know not for what." Fr Shirley Hughson, o.h.c., *Spiritual Letters* (Mowbray).

[1] W. H. Auden, *The Age of Anxiety* (Faber), p. 43.
[2] Karen Horney, *The Neurotic Personality of our Time*, p. 284.
[3] *The Spirit*, ed. B. H. Streeter, p. 114.

valuable and potent influences that we possess for producing that harmony and peace, and that confidence of soul which is needed to bring health and power to a large proportion of nervous patients". Here lies, then, a vast area where the priest can be of immense help to afflicted souls caught up as they are in the uncertainty and whirl of our modern existence, for the priest is as much a therapist in his own right as the doctor or psychiatrist.

There are three important spheres in which the Church can play a vital role. The first is in the realm of *preventive care*. It is the priest who is involved in the life situations of the family: birth, marriage, sickness, and bereavement. He is very often the only person, outside the family and relations, who knows the parishioner long enough to have some idea of his general behaviour and reactions. If the priest is a true pastor, it is he who first observes the mentally ill, and is therefor responsible for doing something about them. This is brought home forcibly in an article written by a psychologist, in which he states: "As a psychologist onlooker at the Church . . . I am struck by two things: firstly that many ministers do not easily recognize the aberrant for whom ordinary measures are of little avail, and secondly, should they recognize that the problems of some of their communicants are in a different order from that of the majority—then for the most part they have very little to offer."[1]

Every priest should have a workaday knowledge of mental disorders, their diagnosis and therapy, but he must be aware of his limitations, and if he is not sufficiently trained he will refer those who need skilled and specialized help to the appropriate authority. He should, for example, be able to differentiate between circumstances of depression and anxiety due merely to the lack of real faith in God or to a psychological disorder.

He should know the difference between delusions, hallucinations, and obsessions.

[1] Art. by Paul De Becker, "The Search for Mental Health", in the *Church of England Newspaper*, 26 June 1957.

DELUSION

Gillespie in his *Textbook of Psychiatry*, describes a delusion in the following terms: "A delusion is a belief which:

(*a*) is not a true fact,

(*b*) cannot be corrected by an appeal to the reason of the person entertaining it and,

(*c*) is out of harmony with the individual's education and surroundings. . . . The type of individual most likely to have delusions is one who normally shows a suspicious argumentative attitude."

A deluded parishioner will be impervious to reason, and it is most wise not to attempt to argue.

HALLUCINATION

When a person sees a "vision" or hears "a voice", he is said to be having hallucinations.[1] (Dan. 4. 4, 5: "I Nebuchadnezzar was at rest in mine house, and flourishing in my palace: I saw a dream which made me afraid, and the thoughts upon my bed and the visions of my head troubled me.") It is often difficult to differentiate between an hallucination and an illusion, i.e. a false perception in the absence of any sensation. The "voices" heard can be of a bizarre kind and provoke the person to acts of violence either against himself or other people.

OBSESSION

A feeling of compulsion to do, say, or think a certain thing. This exists in a mild form in normal people—to walk on the

[1] The great similarities between the "visions" and "voices" of some people who have had hallucinations and the experiences of the saints have often been commented upon, e.g., St Paul saw a blinding flash and heard voices; St Francis of Assisi heard voices and saw visions; St Joan and St Bernadette heard voices.

One of the fundamental differences appears to be that the stature and personality of the saints were well above those of normal men and women. As a result also of their visions they were transformed in character. The spiritual experiences of the saints came from God. Those of the mentally ill are hallucinations with no objective stimulus.

pavement cracks, touch the lamp-posts, etc. In a severe form this type of symptom may become troublesome, and the compulsive feelings, which are realized to be ridiculous, cannot be suppressed without severe anxiety resulting.

If the priest is to play a part in preventive care he should be able to recognize some of the milder symptoms of incipient mental disorder so that he can help or advise before it becomes obvious and disabling. The division between the normal and the abnormal is very thin, and makes mental illness extremely difficult to diagnose in its early stages. Jung pointed out that the most important feature about the neurotic is that he is so normal, suffering simply from more exaggerated forms of emotional conflict which are common to us all. Again, symptoms only have their full meaning and significance when linked up with the whole life-history and general clinical setting.

A person may be mentally ill, and yet be very sensible in his conversation. He may clearly understand all the priest says to him, and yet be mentally ill. When Peer Gynt visited a psychiatric hospital of his time he found it extremely hard to believe that the people there were mentally ill. They talked so sensibly and discussed plans with precision and concern. He spoke to the doctor about it. "They're mad", said the doctor. "They talk sensibly, I admit, but it's all about themselves. They are, in fact, most intelligently obsessed with self. It's all self—morning, noon, and night.[1] We can't get away from it here. We lug it along with us, even through our dreams. Oh yes, young sir, we talk sensibly; but we're mad right enough!"

His memory and comprehension may be normal, his answers sensible, yet his depression can endanger his life. His excitability can annoy others, and his delusions and hallu-

---

[1] *Cf.* "Research shows that patients in mental hospitals use 'I' oftener than any other word—about once every 12 words, three times as often as normal people. As these patients recover, their use of 'I' and 'they' goes down, and their use of 'we' goes up." From "Your Words can tell too Much", by J. K. Lagemann, *Reader's Digest* (September 1961), p. 136.

cinations make him behave abnormally. Indeed, the priest will find that many will deny there is anything wrong with them, and be much annoyed when treatment is advised. Unfortunately many will be found unwilling to consult a psychiatrist, fearing they may be sent to hospital. The priest must stress the importance of early treatment, for then the illness can often be alleviated and cured by attendance at one of the out-clinics or psychiatric centres. If further treatment is advised, the patient need have no fear, for new and successful techniques have been introduced in recent years, and there is a much higher rate of recovery and a more rapid turnover of patients. For example, nine out of ten of those admitted today are discharged within one year, half of them within six weeks, and 92·93% of patients are voluntary.

The priest must be quite honest with the patient, and not try to deceive him if he has to be admitted to hospital, for he must keep contact with his parishioner, particularly when he is discharged back into the parish community. People must be taught to get rid of the age-old attitudes towards mental illness of strait jackets and physical restraints, and it is to be earnestly hoped that the public will understand more and more about mental illness and its treatment.

Often the mentally sick will ask why their minds have become so deranged. Mental illness never has just one cause. There are always many factors involved, some of which are known, and others conjectured. We know there is a considerable variety of ways in which different people respond to stressful situations and changes. Constitutional or hereditary factors predispose some people towards certain symptoms of mental illness. In childhood we all acquire a characteristic mode of response to stress situations. This personality structure does affect our ability to respond to change and stress during the later periods of life. Disturbed social relationships in family or work, in church life, etc., can limit our capacity to stand up to difficulties and stress. Physical factors, such as brain damage, obviously impair our ability to deal with stress and strain. The following milder symptoms should be noted by the priest.

CHANGE IN BEHAVIOUR

A neat and efficient housewife may suddenly become slovenly in her home and in appearance. A serious, respected member of the congregation may suddenly become quarrelsome, and talk and act obscenely. A quiet soul accustomed to retiring to bed early suddenly persists in staying up until the early hours of the morning.

In most examples, the person will not be aware of the sudden change in his behaviour, and may become resentful and antagonistic when it is remarked upon. It is important to realize that these symptoms are not "just stupidity", or a "lot of nonsense". They are deeply significant expressions of the inner life of the person. They are often expressing blind attempts to resolve the problems and conflicts that the person is experiencing within himself. The real cause is often deep down below the surface.

PERIODS OF CONFUSION AND LOSS OF MEMORY

The mentally ill person may have repeated bouts of forgetfulness. He may be at a loss to tell you who he is, where he is, or what is happening.

UNREALISTIC AND BIZARRE IDEAS

He may complain that the people with whom he works are plotting against him. His fellow worshippers are whispering about him in church, or in one of the parochial organizations. The vicar appears to be preaching at him and him alone in his sermons, etc.

Many will have "fixed ideas", and no amount of argument will relieve such a person's despair that he has committed the "unforgivable sin", or that he is going to die before the day is out. He may become aggressive in his attitude to other people because of such unfounded thoughts, for he will naturally feel justified in his suspicions.

SYMPTOMS RELATING TO THE FIVE PRINCIPAL SENSES

He may see things that you know do not exist. He may smell strange odours, and have a horrible taste in his mouth because he thinks people are poisoning his food. With the utmost sincerity he will tell you he is listening to "voices" talking to him. Merely to tell him that they are completely imaginary will do little good, for he will obviously resist the suggestion that it is "just imagination".

GRANDIOSE IDEAS

He may think he is some most famous or important religious or political leader, or even Jesus Christ himself. He will tell you he is going to buy a fleet of the most expensive cars, or purchase a large mansion, which you know to be quite beyond his financial resources.

REPETITIVE ACTS

The mentally sick person will often have a morbid fear of germs and dirt, and will want to carry out repetitive acts, such as hand washing.

FEARS OF BODILY CHANGES

He may be convinced he is suffering from a fatal illness, e.g. carcinoma. He will suffer from symptoms just as much or nearly as much as if they were actually caused by some such disease. Reassurance can help a little, but in most instances skilled and expert help is needed.

ACUTE DEPRESSION

We all suffer from bouts of depression at some time or other, but acute depression is prolonged and makes the individual feel utterly worthless, and he has a more profound disruption of personality than "just a fit of the blues". He will sit for hours without moving or speaking. If he does speak it is often to give vent to complaints of overwhelming worthlessness, and sometimes may even think of suicide.

Many a priest will be well aware that probably quite a number of his parishioners display features of one or other of the above symptoms. It is only when they become exaggerated and prolonged or when there is a sudden outburst that he need be concerned, and then it is often wise to get expert help. With a knowledge of the milder symptoms of mental illness, the priest is now prepared to learn a little more of the history of his parishioner. This he can do by collecting as discreetly as possible useful data about the past and present history of the illness. For example:

(a) When did the parishioner or his friends first think something was wrong? What were the symptoms?

(b) Had there been worry? Loss of sleep? How long? Was there adequate basis for anxiety or grief?

(c) What changes were there in behaviour, in mood, in attitude towards others and towards work?

It should be stressed, however, that many a parish priest will first come up against his parishioner's problems not so much in what he learns about their symptoms as in the unhappiness that their attitudes and behaviour create in the home and family life.

Today many forces storm the bulwark of family life. For example, the priest will meet the young mother who prefers the cash and excitement of "a job in town" to staying at home and looking after her children. There is the father who cannot spare a moment for the family and the children, for his nose must be perpetually at the grindstone, whether it be office or parish. There is the neurotically over-possessive mother, and the over-strict and pious father, etc. So many families live in a state bordering on panic, and with the atmosphere in their homes like "a perpetual pneumatic drill". Often father and mother keep "on the go" so much that there is no time for them to sit and discuss mutual domestic problems. They have nothing in common except the terrible tension in which they live.

Such disorders in inter-personal relationships are also

evident in the life of the parish. There is the member of the congregation who tries to dominate and monopolize the discussion in every meeting; the "hungry for praise, eager for recognition" personality; the hypersensitive parishioner who is always feeling offended and slighted.

The priest should recognize that such difficult parishioners are not "problems" or "nuisances", but people with problems who need to be understood. Aggressiveness, self-pity, suspicion, resentment, anger, avoidance of responsibility—all these can be characteristic of deep-seated neuroses.[1]

Each stage of life—adolescence, courtship, marriage, parenthood, climacteric, and old age—brings its respective problems and gives much scope for pastoral work by an experienced priest. "When I was a child, I spake as a child, I understood as a child . . . but when I became a man, I put away childish things. . . ." (1 Cor. 13. 11.) There are many for whom this saying is untrue, for they continue to be dependent and helpless throughout life. The "childish things"—helplessness, dependency—if carried over to an excessive degree can be socially destructive. The priest will find many other unfortunate characteristics in his parishioners which it is easy to trace back to childhood days, e.g. excessive vanity, self-love, inability to form tender and lasting attachments. These all tend to disrupt good inter-personal relationships,

---

[1] "The Church's Ministry of Healing": Report of Archbishops' Commission, 1958 (C.I.B.), Sections 140, 141:

" 'Disorders of Behaviour.' . . . The Commission wishes to refer especially to the treatment of one class of disorder with which the psychiatrist is often concerned. There is a group of disorders of behaviour the symptoms of which include bad temper, jealousy, resentment, self-pity, grievances and defeatism which, while in the sphere of moral behaviour, may be beyond the control of the will. They may be regarded as differing from 'sins' in the usual sense of the word in that they are the fruit of psychological disorder. Such conditions can be and frequently are, cured by religious conversion. They can also be cured by psychotherapy . . . although not all would agree. There is a growing body of opinion among psychiatrists that these disorders, being in the moral sphere, may require the ministrations of an experienced priest for a complete solution of the patient's whole problem. . . ."

and are responsible for much tragedy and disruption in home and family life.

The problem of the priest is how to deal with these emotionally infantile and irrational personalities, for they need to learn how to develop emotionally, as well as physically and spiritually. The most harmful attitude towards them is neglect, indifference, or harshness. The most helpful attitude is that of devotion and love, not a mere sentimental love or sympathy, but a readiness to understand, respect, and encourage.

Often *adolescence* brings with it the special problems of minor forms of delinquency. John has been caught stealing from another boy's locker in school. Tom has been in Court for possessing drugs. Such instances might be multiplied many times in the regular pastoral rounds of the priest.

It is not an easy task to relate the Christian Faith to such concrete problems of teen-age tensions. The urge to moralize is strong, but if the priest is to be of the maximum help in preventive care he must have a knowledge of the dynamics of such behaviour and how relationships between parent and child can be so disrupted as to lead on to such anti-social behaviour. He must be aware of the more common characteristics underlying much of adolescent delinquency. The child is often unloved and neglected. He feels he is not really wanted by his parents who have little or no understanding of his needs. More often than not there has been a severe disturbance in early relationships between mother and child. Many delinquents are rebels against the severe and rigid authority of over-severe parents. Some have not been helped to grow into mature citizens, for they have been over-protected and "smother-loved" by their parents.

Unfortunately the priest is seldom called in until the situation has become acute. Feelings of guilt and anxiety run high, and these must be dealt with first if the priest is to give the maximum amount of spiritual help. Such factors as television, horror and gangster films, bad company, etc., are sought to externalize the problem, for in this way parents can tactfully avoid facing the real tensions in family relationships which are so often the real root of the trouble. As discreetly as possible it is the task of the priest to direct the attention of the parents inwardly to the everyday running of the home, its disagreements and tensions.

Every child has the longing to be loved, to be important, and to have his needs and wishes taken seriously. Much failure will be experienced in compelling the child to obey the parent's demands, to meet the parent's needs, and to satisfy the parent's wishes. Each child must be understood as a separate and individual personality, known, respected, and loved, and so be able to develop into an adult who can cope with the stress of modern living.

Minor difficulties must be seen primarily as symptoms of faulty personality and character development. To understand and provide spiritual "first aid" the priest must be concerned with the underlying issues and not merely with symptoms. The most important factor seems to be the adolescent's reaction to the other members of the family. When such interpersonal relationships are fraught with tension, anxiety, and strain, the youngster is brought up in an atmosphere of emotional insecurity which so often breeds delinquency. As this problem centres on the functions of and relationship within the family, the Church should be able to offer something of the understanding, respect, and love, which the disturbed adolescent fails to find in his home atmosphere. His one great need is to be accepted.

It cannot be over-emphasized what an important role in preventive care the Church can play by her programme in religious education and group activities for both young and old. Again, much can be done in confirmation instruction, and in preparation for marriage and the setting up of the home. Prevention starts at birth. If the basic desires and needs of the infant are not satisfied, his whole organism can be affected, and his emotional life gets out of balance. Young children, especially those nearing the period of puberty, require special pastoral care from their priest, so that they may

be the more easily enabled to pass through this vital stage of
their lives without psychical tension. A child needs all the
self-confidence he can muster. His questions about sex must
be answered directly and honestly. He will then understand
that sex is not something wrong or sinful, and his curiosity
will be satisfied. It is the family which is the crucial group,
and the happy family, united by ties of affection and companionship, is one of the greatest resources for good mental
health. In the broken home lies the problem; in the happy
and united home is often found the answer.

The changes of *middle age* bring with them significant
emotional involvements, and many mental breakdowns begin
at this period of life. Many of these originate from disillusionment, emptiness, and frustration. Often the children of the
family are married, and the house seems silent and still.
There is disillusionment with life, coupled with guilt over the
past and fear of the future. Herein is a spiritual challenge
which the priest must be prepared to meet. He can guide
those in this stage of life towards helpful and meaningful contact with others sharing similar problems. He can lead them
into intellectual activity and study, into prayer and meditation. He can teach them to number their days and apply their
hearts unto wisdom (Ps. 90. 12).

The problems of *old age* have become complicated by the
fact that we live in an acquisitive society where men are
valued for their productivity. The Christian religion, however, sees man as the child of God, created in the image of
God. Man is seen as someone who can be creative in terms of
human values even when he can no longer be productive in
economic values.

There is a steady increase in the admission rate of old
people to psychiatric hospitals. Little over a decade ago there
were 45,000 aged over sixty-five. At the present time there
are 51,000. Almost 50 per cent of the beds in psychiatric hospitals are occupied by women aged over sixty-five. In his
pastoral care the priest should understand the more common
behaviour patterns of old age as well as some of the causative

factors behind them. If he is alert, he will then understand and appreciate the significance of the lessening of physical vigour, and the frequent threat of economic insecurity.

Childish old people are to be found in every parish, thirsting for love, affection, and a sense of belonging. The priest by his pastoral visits and counselling can show them that the Church does really care. Once the priest understands the psychology of old age, he can make effective use of older people in his parochial programme, and so save them from the greatest agony of all—feeling unwanted or forgotten.

Although it may sound strange to refer to preventive work in regard to old age, yet nevertheless the priest can help young people to prepare for it. Many people never think seriously about this stage of life until it has begun to interefere and restrict their physical or mental structure. The young will also learn to have patient understanding with their ageing parents and old people in general. "My son, help thy father in his age . . . and if his understanding fail, have patience with him. . . ." (Ecclus. 3. 12, 13).

Such an outline can only be partial, and is merely intended to help the priest in his initial dealings with the mentally sick parishioner, and enable him to play a vital role in preventive care. The priest should know when the parishioner requires the attention of a competent psychiatrist, and this referral can only be done through contact with the general practitioner.

In order to help forward preventive care, the Church should provide counselling centres, preferably in the larger parish churches of the provinces. It is essential, too, for the priest to be familiar with the psychiatric and medical services in the neighbourhood. There should also be at least one experienced priest in every diocese to whom special cases may be sent.

Fortunately today there are more and more opportunities being offered to help the pastor to understand some of the deeper conflicts which torment the mind of the mentally ill and how best he can minister to their needs. With a thorough insight into some of the minor mental disorders, coupled with a knowledge of the fundamental tenets of pastoral care and pastoral counselling, the clergy can function in a real *therapeutic role*.[1] However, he will be wise to recommend treatment by a psychiatrist when some of the symptoms mentioned above persist, and when a "spiritual problem" arises revealing a long-standing personality disorder which his pastoral ministry has been unable to influence. He should never hesitate to refer a parishioner in this way, for it is always the wiser course to seek competent and skilled help. After all, referral does not mean desertion, for the priest can continue his pastoral counselling, particularly with the members of the family.

The Institute of Religion and Medicine (58A Wimpole Street, London, W.1) and the various organizations to which its members belong has done much through its "field-groups" to bring together small groups of general practitioners, clergy, psychiatrists, social workers, etc., in which mutual trust and confidence can be fostered between members of what has become known as the "caring professions". Working alongside one another, each can contribute towards the health and healing of the mentally afflicted. The psychiatric hospital chaplain who has been trained can take his rightful place in the therapeutic team and participate in the treatment programme, for in attempting to bring healing to the whole personality of the patient he is inevitably involved in the psycho-therapeutic process.

The third important role the Church can play is in the community and the *after-care* of the discharged patient, for the priest can be the liaison between the patient and the outside community. The 1959 Mental Health Act threw greater responsibility on the local authorities and gradually more and more patients are discharged back into the community. There is still however an acute shortage of suitable residen-

---

[1] For a full and important study of the therapeutic role the reader is referred to *Clinical Theology*, Dr Frank Lake (Darton, Longman & Todd).

tial accommodation in the community where there can be an adequate degree of supervision away from the hospital environment. In the House of Commons (1967) the following statement was made by Bernard Braine: "I have heard it suggested and never denied that there may be as many as 25,000 old people in psychiatric hospitals who could be discharged tomorrow if there were someone at home to care for them. It has been estimated that half of the 64,000 mentally subnormal patients in hospital might live in the community if there were suitable accommodation and support found for them." Day hospitals have been established, where patients either spend the whole or part of the day, returning home in the evening or, vice versa, do a job of work by day and reside in the hostel by night. The Church can offer valuable help here in supplementing the work which is being done in such centres. In close co-operation with the hospital the priest can help in the further rehabilitation of the patient by introducing him to the supportive fellowship of the parish community, and its group activities. He can also help the family in their dealings with the patient.[1]

The link between the parish church and the local psychiatric hospital should be as strong as possible. Selected patients might be encouraged to attend meetings of the various church organizations. They, in turn, would visit patients in hospital, particularly those who are friendless, working in full co-operation with the hospital's League of Friends. Activities might be arranged for patients both inside the hospital, e.g. concerts, social clubs, drama groups, and outside, e.g. taking patients home, shopping, visiting them after discharge, or raising money for extra amenities.

Many experiments are already in progress for providing support within the community for those who are mentally ill. The colony of Gheel in Belgium has shown that a number of mentally ill patients living and working in the community

[1] See *The Role of the Churches in the Care of the Elderly*, Report, National Old People's Welfare Council, 1968.

need not be socially disrupting. In this small agricultural village approximately 2,500 mental patients live in the community with the farmers and their families, and there is complete lack of segregation. Maintenance of human dignity as a social entity and a part of a family, and the possibility of useful employment all play a vital therapeutic role in the rehabilitation of the mentally sick. The value of the treatment available in the finest hospital with the most modern psychiatric facilities is questioned if the patient is returned to the home or community whose limitations contributed in no small measure to his disability. If the needs of the patient are interpreted to members of the community, the priest with others, e.g. the psychiatrist, social worker, and the social agencies in the community, can learn of such needs and limitations and so work with him towards full recovery.

When the psychiatric patient is discharged he does not need to be treated with any special care or in any abnormal way. What he does need is love and friendship. It must be remembered that his environment is now very different from what it was when he was in hospital. Let him know that the parish is glad to have him back once more in its fellowship. He must not be pampered as an invalid, for in the majority of instances the sooner he resumes his normal place in home and parish the better. With an understanding and accepting approach, he will be helped to regain his self-confidence and to shoulder squarely his responsibilities once more. It is often useful to consult the psychiatrist as to the best way of assisting the particular individual. A church with a deep sense of fellowship and family worship can do much for the former patient, for the fundamental anxiety of the human spirit is "separation anxiety", the feeling of being cut off from the reality of his own true self, of his neighbour, and of his God. Unfortunately, the conventional social standard implicitly demanded by many church fellowships has taken the place of a living spirit of Christian love, and such an atmosphere only tends to increase the conflict of the emotionally sick person. There is no evidence to prove that fear, anxiety, or guilt is any less common among faithful communicants and members of church organizations than among those outside the ranks of the Church.

Is the Church of today offering the dynamic healing force for the whole man that it should be?[1] Those who study emotional disorder are being led more and more to realize that the real problem underlying so many of the conflicts of the mind is the lack of an inner sense of security—a fear of being unloved. Karen Horney believes all breakdown is due to the disturbance of personal relationships, and this insecurity gives rise to what she describes as "basic anxiety". A kindly word, an out-stretched hand, means a tremendous amount to one who has experienced the loneliness of a mental illness. If the patient has nothing to come back to, he may be alleviated for a time, but he is not likely to remain well.

Unfortunately today shame and stigma are still frequently attached to mental illness. Many fear their discharge out into a world which is still far too full of chatter and unkind gossip about the mentally afflicted. The priest, however, works not as a lone figure but as a member of the Body of Christ, and needs to have the congregation behind him to offer to the discharged patient the same acceptance and understanding given to the physically ill. Both priest and congregation work together to develop an understanding of the real difficulties which the neurotic person faces in the Church and in the world around him. He needs kindness, understanding, and freedom from the judgement of others. The more naturally and normally he is treated the better, and the approach to him will be generally the same as our approach to the normal personality.

In the New Testament the Church is more than a collection of individual persons; it is the Family of God in which all members are loved and cared for, in which joys and sorrows are shared. The Church today should be that sharing redemp-

---

[1] A most useful pamphlet outlining the Church as a therapeutic community is D. V. Martin, *The Church a Healing Community* (The Guild of Health).

tive fellowship in which those who are strong should bear the infirmities of the weak (Rom. 15. 1), in which, when one member suffers, all members suffer (1 Cor. 12. 26; Gal. 6. 1). Instead, it seems to have lost its sense of "Koinonia", and what has happened to the Church has had effect on the average church member. In an atmosphere of inter-personal isolation, personality problems so often develop. Those who have problems seem alone in the midst of people. "Where the enthusiasm of the early church is still alive or has been reborn within Christendom, where the Gospel is truly preached, and the Sacraments truly received", writes Stinnette,[1] "the Christian Community is a reality that stands as a strong bulwark against subversive anxiety. This is a recorded fact in the clinical experience of an ever-growing number of psychiatrists and counsellors who have concerned themselves with the relation of Christianity to health. . . . Love is the reality of the Christian 'Koinonia' but its source is God, and not the good-will of men. Within that community, a power is available to live through every affliction—'imprisonments, tumults, labours'—with quiet confidence."

[1] Charles Stinnette, *Anxiety and Faith*, p. 143.

2

The Priest as Pastoral Counsellor

> A Minister is not only for public preaching, but to be a
> known counsellor for their souls, as the lawyer is for their
> estates, and the physician for their bodies; so that each
> man that is in doubts and straits, should bring his case to
> him and desire resolution. . . .   RICHARD BAXTER
>
> And his name shall be called . . . Counsellor.   Isa. 9. 6
>
> Give thy servant therefore an understanding mind to
> govern thy people.   1 Kings 3. 9 (R.S.V.)

As we read through the Gospels we find that over and over
again our Lord's attitude to the individual is stressed. He
always treated people as being each one uniquely important.
In his busy life he always had time to devote to their needs.
To help people individually may seem to so many slow,
tedious, and time-absorbing—and indeed it is!—but it is the
primary charge laid upon every priest at his ordination. The
door of his study should always be open to the burdened
parishioner, and his mind also should be alert to the human
problems before him. He may have to possess a patience
which is greater than Job's, but he will have won the confidence of his parishioner, which will eventually lead to a real
understanding of his problems and difficulties. In this way
the priest can make a most valuable contribution to the
spiritual and mental health of the people committed to his
charge.

It was Fosdick who once said that a man is like an island.
Sometimes you have to row around him before you find a
place to land. There are some people who present a wall of

indifference, some a barrier of apathy, and others a defence of hostility. We have to keep on paddling until we find the best place to land, and it is usually on the beach of some definite human need.

There is a persistent demand in these days of mechanized society for a more effective pastoral ministry, for we seem to be losing the art of personal and individual dealing with anxious and distressed souls. Oh, that we might recapture a little of the spirit of a St Francis "who deliberately did not see the mob for the men.... He only saw the image of God multiplied but never monotonous. To him a man was always a man and did not disappear in a dense crowd any more than in a desert ... there was never a man who looked into those brown burning eyes without being certain that Francis Bernadone was really interested in him; in his own inner individual life from the cradle to the grave; that he himself was being valued and taken seriously."[1]

The general insecurity of the world today heightens the personal insecurity of each individual. The tensions of the external world are indicative of the many strains within man himself. Jung was once asked by one of his patients: "Dr Jung, how do you keep your patience with us and our puny problems, when Europe is falling apart and you have work of world importance?" Jung replied: "Because the world problems start with individuals." On all sides our people cry out for help, and John Henry Newman might well have been describing our modern predicament when he wrote: "How many souls are there in distress, anxiety, and loneliness, whose one need is to find a being to whom they can pour out their feelings unheard by the world. They want to tell them; and not to tell them; they wish to tell them to one who is strong enough to hear them, and yet not too strong to despise them."

Our ministry to the individual seems to be caught up in the rush and speed of the age. We appear too busy to see people,

[1] G. K. Chesterton, *St Francis of Assisi* (Hodder & Stoughton), p. 110. Quoted by Paul Tournier in *The Meaning of Persons*, p. 183.

and consequently they fail to contact us because they feel we are too preoccupied with other things which are more important. "These clever men are all so stupid, there's no one for me to talk to . . . always alone, alone. I haven't a soul . . . and who I am, and why I am, nobody knows," cries Charlotta in Chekhov's *The Cherry Orchard*. This pressure of other things can so easily lead to pastoral work which so seldom reaches the roots of human problems.

The secret of the priest's ministry to the individual may be seen as a triangle—God at the top, priest and individual below, both in touch with God and with one another through him. If he is to help people he must be humble, and true humility begins with his continued awareness that it is not he who helps, but the Holy Spirit who works in and through each one of us. When the priest fails he may be certain that he has put far too much of himself in the picture. He is in the picture, and yet so scarcely there, so completely should he be eclipsed in the presence of Christ himself, the great helper of human souls.

Often today we see the cure of souls passing more and more out of the hands of the priest, and the pastoral field being encroached upon by other professions. It has been suggested that the reasons for this lie in the fact that people prefer to look for physical causes of their difficulties. If a physical cause is found, the patient is thus saved the necessity of facing up to the realities of his inner life. Cause in the body is less disturbing to him than a cause in his character. He has the lurking fear that the priest may preach, pray, or pass moral judgement. The vast prestige of modern science mantles the psychiatrist, and the patient approaches him with high hopes. Allport suggests that people are not uninfluenced by the united front presented by science as compared with the divided sects of Christendom.

There is also the quite false idea in many people's minds that religious people should not have problems and that their difficulties are all due to lack of faith on their part. This prevents them seeking the help of their priest. A few fear that what they discuss might get around the parish.[1] With others a sense of pride compels them to keep things to themselves. Again, there are many who see the father-image in their priest, and his role of authority proves a barrier to free and easy conversation. They feel they must say the sort of things their priest would like to hear, or that he will be shocked and offended at some of their problems.

On the other hand, as soon as parishioners feel that their priest is knowledgeable, sympathetic, and available, more and more will be prepared to bring their difficulties to him. It is often useful to make known in the parish magazine or through announcements in church that the parish priest is available at certain times in either the vicarage or the church vestry. Many difficulties and problems can be observed by the priest in the confessional, and there can follow the suggestion that these might be talked over at length later. Each priest will be able to gauge his time-table and keep a correct balance between his counselling periods and other important aspects of his ministry, for counselling is just part of his total task— just one of his many duties.[2]

What is pastoral counselling? It must first of all be distinguished from the giving of advice or information. In many instances the priest will be called upon to give guidance and tell people what to do, for he is priest first and counsellor second. But this method does not always work, for certain people will not take or follow the advice. Counselling then becomes necessary with its emphasis on self-understanding

[1] Nothing is more devastating to the whole counselling programme of the priest than the reputation of not being able to keep information confidential.

[2] "Pastoral counselling is to be considered as part of the larger domain of pastoral care, which is the chief work of the clergyman. . . . I consider this care to be first of all a spiritual nature and to be exercised through the spiritual ministrations of the priest . . . there are some clergymen who have become so enthusiastic about counselling . . . that though they have become good counsellors, I doubt that they are longer functioning as clergymen". William C. Bier, s.j., *Pastoral Psychology*, February 1959, p. 7.

and insight by the parishioner, rather than merely being told what to do. The successful stages of counselling depend on how much self-understanding the parishioner obtains, not whether or not he takes advice. He is encouraged to make decisions for himself.

It must also be distinguished from psychotherapy, for this method lies in the domain of the psychiatrist or psycho-therapist, and is highly technical, dealing as it does with the diagnosis and treatment (non-physical) of mental illness. In *no circumstances* should the priest become involved in psychotherapeutic techniques when ministering to his people unless he is fully trained.

Counselling then is more than the giving of advice or in-formation and yet is not so deep and intricate as psycho-therapy. The people seen in counselling are not as deeply disturbed as those seen in psychotherapy. Again, counselling is always carried on through the conscious level, and the pastoral counsellor should only be interested in this con-scious, verbal plane. Neurotic personalities should always be referred to those who are skilled and competent to deal with them, for the priest should never attempt to work alone with the severely emotionally disturbed.

Pastoral counselling is not counselling in the psychiatric sense, although there are some common features. It is rather counselling in a spiritual framework and perspective. It is in other words three-dimensional—Holy Spirit, priest, and parishioner. Curran distinguishes the unique characteristics of *pastoral counselling* by emphasizing that "the person has come for personal help certainly, but he has come, too, to re-organize not only his relationship with himself and others but his relationship with God . . . the background is the Divine. He is looking at himself not only as he or others may see and judge him, but as God sees and judges him. This deep and significant additional force lies behind everything he says to the counsellor. Here clearly is a definable distinction that is peculiar to the religious counsellor. Interwoven in the fabric of this pastoral counselling relationship is always a theological design. . . . It is not two but a Third who shares intimately in this pastoral counselling relationship . . . the pastoral counsellor . . . spends himself for others in such a way that God's grace and their own reasonable insights may be productive of a more adequate psychological and spiritual integration in time and eternity."[1]

There are two approaches in counselling—the directive and the non-directive or "client-centred". The first emphasizes appeal to reason. Case-histories, psychological tests, and diagnoses are all used. The second, which is more applicable for the priest, stresses the feelings and attitudes of the person counselled, and the passive role of the counsellor.

Directive counselling has been defined as "the process of helping the individual to analyse his own problem so that he knows what it really is, to consider possible means of solution, to provide him with necessary information so that he can think intelligently about his problem, and then *guide* him through a process of thinking so that he eventually finds a solution or at least a constructive programme of action that he accepts as his own".

In directive counselling every effort should be made by the priest to ascertain the resources which are available to the parishioner both *within himself* and *in the environment* of which he is a part. He should constantly attempt to get all the facts which it is reasonably possible to attain. After the priest has enabled the parishioner to discuss openly all phases which are related to his situation, and all of the facts are obtained which can be obtained, the time has come for him to guide the person in the processes of facing the integral factors involved.

The third stage is reached when the parishioner is brought to the realization that he is about to proceed *on his own initiative and will power* in carrying out the implications of his new perspective, and the decision at which the counselling process has helped him to arrive.

---

[1] C. A. Curran, "A Catholic Psychologist looks at Pastoral Counselling". Art. in *Pastoral Psychology*, February 1959, p. 28.

The final phase is a positive and personal statement by the counsellor which is of a reassuring nature. It should be clear, brief, and simple, and it should be as convincing as we can make it.

Directive counselling is helpful because nearly everyone is suggestible. Many problems are mental conflicts, and consequently whatever can influence mental conditions can bring about a resolution or an alleviation of the conflict. Good suggestions of whatever nature they may be, whether they are made directly or indirectly, openly or under cover, are most beneficial psychic influences. Interest, esteem, admiration, praise, gratitude, encouragement, contain strong elements of suggestion for good. On the other hand, negative suggestions can be very harmful, e.g. contempt, scorn, ridicule, irony, etc.

For this method the most useful responses of the counsellor would be those of approval and encouragement, e.g. "That's fine". In other words, any statement which lends emotional support or approval to the security of the individual is helpful. There will be the giving of information or explanation about any questions on the nature of behaviour, i.e. anything which is recognized as a generally established fact. Persuasion will be used to convince the individual that he should accept the counsellor's point of view, e.g. "Don't you think it would be better that way, now?" In the directive method of counselling there will be both disapproval and criticism. There will be interpretation with attempts to indicate why the person involved does or feels something, e.g. "When people feel frustrated, they often act the way you do. There's your problem!"

The second approach is that of non-directive or "client-centred" therapy.[1] According to Rogers, self-concept is one of the most important features of this method. As a person matures he has an idea of himself, i.e. self-concept. At the

---

[1] The founder of this "client-centred" approach is Carl R. Rogers, and for further study of his theories and methods the reader is referred to his *Counselling* and *Psychotherapy*, and his later work *Client-centred Therapy*.

same time he has an idea of what he really is, i.e. concept of reality. If these two concepts are congruent the result is a well-adjusted individual. In so far as they are apart, and self-concept does not coincide with reality or the world of experience, the result is a maladjusted or sick person.

In the non-directive method the counsellor tries to help the individual experience the world of reality and bring it into congruence with self-concept. The aim is to help the person explore his self-concept. If the counsellor wants to do this, he must begin by seeing the world as if through the eyes of the person being helped. He must share his experience and feelings. This demands full acceptance of the individual, taking him as he is, with no conditions and no "ifs" or "buts". The person is then not afraid to express everything, even to the point where he becomes aware of things of which he was not aware before, and expresses these.

The person, the individual, must take the initiative, for this approach emphasizes the important factor that he can solve his own problems under the proper conditions. It is these conditions that the counsellor tries to provide.

The real purpose of this method, then, is to create an atmosphere in which the person being helped can feel completely at ease, completely free to express any feeling, any thought, or any emotional response of which he is or has been aware.

Non-directive counselling aims directly toward the greater independence and integration of the individual, rather than hoping that such results will accrue if the counsellor assists in solving the problem. The aim is to help the individual *grow*, so that he can cope with the present problem and with later problems that arise, in a better integrated fashion. It relies on the individual's drive toward growth, health, and adjustment.

It lays great stress upon emotional elements. Most maladjustments are not the result of failure to know the intellectual aspects, but are the result of the blocking of certain emotional satisfactions—the feeling aspects of the situation. It lays great stress on the immediate situation, and does not delve into the individual's past any more than is necessary.

Non-directive counselling sees the counselling relationship as a growth experience. Other methods expect the individual to grow and change and make better decisions *after* he leaves the interview. This method helps the individual learn to understand himself, make significant independent choices, and act maturely. In other words, it is not a preparation for change—it *is* change.

For this method the most useful responses by the counsellor would be simple acceptance, e.g. "Yes", "M-mm", "I see", "That's right". Unlike directive counselling, the priest's responses must not imply approval or criticism. There will be restatement of the content of the problem in the form of a simple repeating of what the parishioner has said, without any efforts to organize, clarify, or interpret it, or any effort to show that the counsellor is appreciating the feeling of the parishioner's statement by understanding it.

Statements by the counsellor will put the individual's feeling or affective tone in somewhat clearer and more recognizable form, e.g. "It makes you feel very much annoyed", "You love your mother but you resent her telling you what to do". Paul Johnson in his *Pastoral Ministration*[1] has summed up the difference between the directive and non-directive approach in the following terms: "A directive counsellor takes control of the interview by asking leading questions to conduct his own investigation along the lines of his interest and gain the information he considers important. . . . He takes the authoritative role that he knows what is best for the person before him. He proceeds to choose the goals that the person has been unable to choose for himself, and to advise him how best to move towards them. . . ." In contrast, "a non-directive counsellor places responsibility upon the person to lead the conversation according to his interests, tell him what he is ready to admit, discover his own

[1] Op. cit., pp. 78, 79.

insights, choose his own goals, and decide what steps he will take in looking toward them . . .".

In his pastoral counselling there are certain attitudes that the priest can assume. He may give commands and rules, and adopt an authoritative role. Generally speaking this authoritative attitude is ineffective and meets with resistance. It can, however, be most helpful when ministering to those with scruples. Again, the priest may exhort or persuade. This may be effective for mild disturbances. Perhaps the oldest and most common approach is that of suggestion. It sometimes works so long as there is not a deep emotional problem. But at best it is superficial treatment and is not really helpful for acute problems. Many priests tend to use intellectual interpretation. This can often be helpful, but only after the person has been prepared and is ready to accept it. Merely to tell someone that he is suffering from, for instance, an anxiety neurosis does not help. It may, however, be useful in certain and later stages of counselling, and can be used effectively when the person whom the priest is helping is intelligent, and when there has already been set up an atmosphere of counselling. Probably the best approach for the priest is that of understanding.

Counselling is not dependent upon any particular technique or "bag of tricks", and there is no easy road to becoming a good counsellor. If the priest attempts to make the interview follow a preconceived set of rules or techniques he will soon run into difficulties. He will be thwarted by the fear about what to say, and when and where to say it.

It is important for the priest to know the different types of emotional disorders, for "you cannot judge cases justly unless you know the past lives of your penitents; unless you know them as individuals; unless you are familiar with the reactions, the mental habits, the trains of thought that have made your penitent or your parishioner what he or she is, and what makes him or her different from the other members of the congregation".[1] The priest can then think and pray with his

---

[1] J. R. Oliver, *Psychiatry and Mental Health*, p. 9.

people about their problems as a trusted friend, helping them not only to help themselves, but to find God their saviour and deliverer. This is not to say that no skill is needed, for it is not an easy task to assist people to grow, freeing them for normal growth and development. It needs something far more than "being nice" to someone in trouble.

Some words of Fénelon form an apt description of the whole art of counselling: "The object is to place yourself upon a level with the lowest and most imperfect; to encourage in them a freedom which must make it easy for them to open their heart to you." Or as he wrote in a letter to his niece (19 July 1712): "Speak little; listen much; think far more of understanding hearts and of adapting yourself to their needs, than of saying clever things to them. Show that you have an open mind, and let everyone see by experience that there is safety and consolation in opening his mind to you. . . . Never say more than is needed, but let whatever you do say be said with entire frankness. Let no one fear to be deceived by trusting you. . . . Keep track of all who come to you, and follow them up, if they are disposed to escape. You should become all things to all the children of God, for the sake of gaining every one of them. And correct yourself, for the sake of correcting others."

THE INTERVIEW

First impressions are of tremendous importance. The battle is often won or lost in the first half-hour of the interview. Nothing, not even the smallest movement or change of expression is meaningless or accidental. Even the tone of voice plays a vital part, and we must overcome the tendency to shout at those who are not deaf. God has given us in our voices a wonderful instrument of healing. "As soon as I heard him speak, I knew he would be able to help me!"

The outward appearance and dress of the priest are important. (Avoid the danger of looking like an undertaker!) The study should be clean and bright, symbolizing hope, light, and healing. There should be a comfortable armchair available, and the room should be warm and homely. (How difficult it is to talk about the things of God with cold feet!)[1] Chairs should be side by side rather than directly facing each other, and it is less formal and authoritative if the priest does not interview from behind his desk.

The very fact that the parishioner has come for help is a most significant step. His first need is to talk, not to be talked to, for he cries with the prophet Job: "Oh! that one would hear me!" At this stage the primary task of the priest is to listen, and it is just here that so many of us fail. We have been trained to be talkers! Many priests find it difficult to develop the art of listening as they have for so long been "problem solvers". It is not easy to listen and listen intelligently, but it helps the parishioner to feel accepted and more ready to accept himself. It is not listening in itself which is important, but the attitude in which we listen, for listening is quite different from keeping quiet. The counsellor must be sufficiently interested to listen to his people, and not simply take over and try to solve their problems for them. He must listen and make the sort of reply that reflects rather than comments on the person's feelings. For instance, it is more helpful to respond, "Yes, I can quite understand how you feel", than to state, "You mustn't cry and be upset. Try to be brave. Everything will be all right".

Good and effective counselling allows people, probably for the first time, to talk freely about themselves, and as they grow in confidence and security with the counsellor, to pour forth many deep and hidden things. The priest should not be concerned to try to bring up topics which *he* feels are significant and interesting. After all, it is the parishioner who is the expert on his problem, and he should be left free to state it as he likes, or thinks most helpful. What is said must be kept in strictest confidence, and not used as future sermon material!

[1] I am greatly indebted to the Reverend J. Crowlesmith of the Methodist Society for Medical and Pastoral Psychology for many useful hints in conducting an interview.

We must become what Sullivan describes as "participant observers". The first evidence of skill on the part of the counsellor is when the taciturn and withdrawn are enabled to express themselves and talk about their problems. The priest may get the taciturn parishioner to go deeper into his problem by asking: "How do you mean?" or "Will you please tell me more about that?" They are often excellent devices for getting the person to talk. If people do not talk freely it is so easy to feel the fault must lie with them. It may well be with us.

The first stage is one of "releasing" or "ventilating" problems which up until now the troubled soul has looked upon as unique.

The divulging of material must be left with the parishioner, and with a soul in distress we must not expect a clear chronological sequence of events told to us. It is significant to note what is told first. It can be a mountain peak, yet on the other hand it may be a mere postscript! He must be left to tell his story in his own way, and we ought not to demand more than his capacity. We should rather expect the least from him, and not the most. There is a place for neurosis in the world, and if we deprive a man of it too quickly or in too decisive a manner his last state will be worse than his first. To rob him too quickly of the secondary gain that his illness brings is to set up a psychological crisis. We move together, as two children of the living God, as two people who have walked along part of the same pathway, and fallen into some of the same quagmires. We must never be shocked or surprised at what is said. It is important for the priest to be detached and objective, but not aloof or condescending. This is often far more difficult for the priest who knows the family and its environment, than for the psychiatrist or the psychotherapist who sees the parishioner on a professional basis. But a calm objectivity should be the aim, for we do not help people by entangling ourselves in their problems. Then follows the analysis, when the problems become something outside themselves, and can be analysed and thought about in a new light and with less emotion. Both priest and individual now work together, discovering the source of the problem. This is often most difficult, for the real problem is frequently buried deep beneath a heap of irrelevant statements and actions. Often a smile will cover some underlying hostility and bright chatter will be a camouflage for some underlying depression. The priest should be familiar with the art of asking questions, avoiding those that can only evoke "Yes" or "No". Questions should be suggestive rather than direct, avoiding the tendency of probing. Finally comes the synthesis—an integrated understanding of how the problem came about is acquired from the past and present. God himself now becomes, probably for the first time, a real, loving God, and not a fearsome image from which one must hide.

Interviews should take place in a real spirit of "empathy" —a deep state of identification of personalities. Empathy is the way our Lord looked at people. This meeting of two personalities has been likened to the contact of two chemical substances. If there is any reaction, both are transformed. This atmosphere cannot be forced, but must be allowed to grow slowly and naturally. It must always be achieved.

The parishioner who has come for help must not be treated as a case, but he must be able to feel we have a real personal concern for him and his need. It is easy to find our mind half wandering as we listen, but divided attention (looking at our watch or out of the window, a muffled yawn, etc.) soon breaks *rapport*, and personal interest soon suffers when we are preoccupied with thinking ahead. The slightest trace of irritability or impatience will retard our help, and it is most disturbing to the parishioner if we telephone or open mail in his presence. We must concentrate and not think we know all. It helps tremendously if we make him feel he matters, and we are really interested in him.

We must pray always to be delivered from superiority. It can be a wonderful feeling for our pride to think someone has sought our help. The priest should be interested in personalities as well as in symptoms. "You are the first person I've met for a very long time who is more interested in me than in my rheumatism!"

Throughout the interview we must be observant; watching how the parishioner walks, holds himself, and how he moves his hands and feet, for these are often indicative of the trouble, e.g. fiddling with an engagement or wedding ring. Certainly no woman with an inferiority complex will walk into the study with arms akimbo!

Between interviews the priest should always take ten to fifteen minutes' quiet, for recollection and prayer. General Gordon in one of his letters says that "praying for people ahead of me whom I am about to visit gives me much strength; and it is wonderful how something seems already to have passed between us when I meet a chief, for whom I prayed, for the first time. On this I base my hopes for a triumphant march to Frascher. I have really no troops with me, but I have the Shekinah." If the unseen link was so strong between two strangers, what must it not be between a priest and his people! It used to be said of Osler that, by merely watching a patient walking across the floor, he could tell him what was the matter with him. Such insight on the spiritual plane is reserved only for those who "watch and pray".

In the first interview with a troubled soul the priest should not argue or challenge. If the person does present a distorted view, it is very easy to fall into argument. These tactics are ill-advised, since he needs to maintain his distorted point of view to bolster his defence. To attack this directly exposes him to anxiety, and he may not be able to tolerate such an attack on his defensive system. The priest can throw out such statements as, "Yes, I perfectly understand why you feel this way, but there are other ways of looking at the situation . . .".

There should be no false assurances and false promises. To reassure him may be a futile gesture, although some re-assurance may be attempted where he shows symptoms of underestimating. It is folly to promise results if the priest has no knowing what the course will be. False promises will always boomerang, and if they are not fulfilled all confidence in the priest will be lost. In the early stages of counselling it is wise for the priest not to interpret or speculate on the problem before him. The parishioner is unprepared for speculation until the atmosphere of *rapport* has been established. "It will be necessary to know a little more about your problem before a valid opinion can be passed."

No one should be made to accept help. Once the priest has presented the facts to him then the choice must always be left to him. "Wilt thou be made whole?" The best response is always sympathetic listening, and the joining in any attack the parishioner may launch against the family, or friends, must be avoided at all costs. For example, when a parishioner states "My wife is impossible to live with. She is always nagging away at me", it is not suitable for the priest to remark in response, "How terrible! Doesn't she know how much it affects you?" A far more helpful reply is: "This must naturally upset you. A situation like this could be disturbing to any person, but don't get unduly perturbed about it." The priest should also avoid the tendency to criticize another priest or doctor, no matter how strong the evidence is. One does not know how much the parishioner's story is coloured by misinterpretation or transference.

If you feel a dislike for the person or a prejudice against him, it is always wise to see that he is passed on to some other priest. When we get close enough to the needs of other people, we sometimes step on their toes at some point. The priest must not be put off if the parishioner dislikes him intensely for a while. Never be unduly alarmed at a negative transference. "You're not helping me. I would like to go and see someone else."

It is wise for the priest to fix a therapeutic goal, for it can become so easy to drift along. We ought to know where to stop with some of the people who cling to us, and who never wish to stand on their own two feet. Our aims in counselling are *integration*, *wholeness*, and *maturity*, and no one but the priest can make this contribution to healing. We can lead our people to see that the facing and discarding of their fears and hates is the price of the new life we can hold out to them in Christ. As medicine can be unpleasant, or an operation painful, yet so necessary for the health of the body, so dealing with the problems of our people can be painful in places, but often the pain will be lost in the joy of peace in mind.

The relationship between priest and parishioner is a unique inter-personal experience through which a patient feels a trust, understanding, acceptance, and warmth such as he has not encountered before. What Goldbrunner says about the doctor–patient relationship is also true of the relationship between priest and parishioner: "The coming together of the doctor and the patient creates an atmosphere which in fact proceeds from and is created by the doctor and enwraps the patient. The effect it has on him is usually that he finds himself saying, to his own surprise, things which he has never wanted or has never been able to say owing to various resistances. He feels accepted and at home, moved and sustained by the doctor's vitality. He participates in the doctor's life and this leads to a feeling of confidence, an inclination to discuss sore points, a readiness to show and give himself without a mask. Moreover, this participation in the doctor's world has a constellating force; the problems which oppress the patient come to a head and are prepared for birth as if by the hand of an obstetrician."[1]

The cultivation of *rapport* is the primary objective of the first phase of treatment, for without this the parishioner will not resolve his basic resistance to any exploration of his problem. We may use the useful illustration of salesmanship to illustrate our point. In selling his product the salesman is up against sales resistance. Experience teaches him not to force his sales until that resistance has been broken down, otherwise his approach is fatal. He soon discovers that the best way to resolve resistance is to sell himself to the customer who is then more likely to accept any statements which he

---

[1] Joseph Goldbrunner, *Cure of Mind and Cure of Soul*, p. 87.

may make about the product. In counselling, the counsellor is a special sort of "salesman" out to sell the patient a product, namely a new way of life. In the same way, the priest must win the parishioner's confidence with a friendly approach. He can then go on to help him buttress up his self-mastery, achieve a more adaptable series of relationships with others, and be shorn of all façades. Until this working relationship is established, the parishioner will be unable to challenge the values of his illness. (For some people it is more tolerable to endure physical illness than to face the deeper causes.) This relationship, then, is the prime factor in our counselling with those in difficulties.

Parishioners will utilize counselling in a variety of ways, which are inimical to *rapport*. They will often make themselves dependent upon the priest, and will seek for sympathy and acceptance. They will want to express feelings that tear them from within, which they usually hold in check. The priest must be equipped to accept these strivings and react to them in a therapeutic manner. To do this, the priest must understand the constituents of each of the parishioner's needs.

The parishioner may want to be dependent. The emotionally sick feel helpless and want to be nurtured back to health. There is always great need of dependence. The priest needs great astuteness here in discovering how much help the individual needs, the grading of support according to the severity of the disturbance, and the imposing upon him of as much responsibility as he can take.

Yearnings for understanding and acceptance are part of the social nature of man, and they are all the more urgent in the emotionally sick, who anticipate condemnation and rejection. It is essential that the priest be capable of giving warmth and approval no matter how disturbed the parishioner may be. He must be careful not to smother with cloying kindness. Any personal characteristics in the priest which interfere with this will constitute handicaps in establishing a proper relationship.

Often the parishioner will want to relieve himself of painful feelings and ideas. He has an overwhelming desire to unburden himself of fear or guilt, etc., which will be accompanied by an immediate but temporary relief. The priest must endure these outbursts, and display an objective attitude, neither condemning nor sanctioning.

All those in emotional difficulties will seek a way in which they can act out the tendencies that relate to actual or factual personal images, and will be eager for a transference relationship. This is a projection of feelings which originate in past experiences. There must be an understanding of this mechanism by the priest and he must also be aware of the manifestations of counter-transference.

In counselling, the priest has multiple roles to play. He must first work out his own personal problems and then he will be all the more flexible in his dealings with a variety of parishioners. In order to express his diverse needs the parishioner will strive to force the priest to fulfil these multiple roles. He will be seen as a helping authority, for this is the traditional relationship between the priest and penitent, doctor and patient. The priest will succeed or fail in just the way the parishioner interprets his activity. The disturbed soul will often seek a parental image—a figure who will grant him bounties without stint. This, of course, will vary from parishioner to parishioner, and the intensity of these attitudes will be determined by the early frustrations experienced by him. The interview is much enhanced if the priest fits into the role which the parishioner wants to see.

On the basis of previous experiences the parishioner may project. That is, he will expect to be treated by the priest as he has been treated previously by his parents. In accordance with these expectations and fears, he will accordingly treat and respond to the priest. Illness is a defence, and the healing of illness lies in the illness itself. Under certain circumstances he will act out with the priest what he had already experienced as a child. The priest under these circumstances plays the parallel role of the parent.

4

The priest will be seen as the representative of other important past personages. The priest may be employed as the object on whom there is a transference of attitudes projected to others besides parents, e.g. a brother, sister, teacher, or friend who has played a significant role in the early life of the parishioner.

The priest may be regarded as an individual with whom the parishioner can establish a reliable relationship, and this attitude can be encouraged. There are, however, resistances to an effective relationship and perhaps the most obstinate is the clinging, dependent attitude to the priest. This is rooted in an intense feeling of helplessness on the part of those seeking his help. The parishioner must be weaned from this feeling, and the priest must give a rational reason for refusing this bulk of responsibility. He can explain to the parishioner that by supplying his demands his growth becomes inhibited.

Another disturbing factor is when the individual has fears of the priest being a destructive being who will threaten, or engulf, or punish him for his past maladjustments. As soon as he sees that his revelations of his inner life fail to bring forth resentment he will feel dissatisfied and often want to seek a more active therapist. Often the parishioner will be nonplussed when the attack he expects is not forthcoming, and he will become resentful at the delay of that which he has considered inevitable. He will begin to revaluate the authority of the priest and feelings of warmth and confidence will emerge.

In his dealings with distressed souls, the priest must always allow them to choose their own pace, and must work slowly, steadily, and prayerfully along with the parishioners. Very often the priest can be put off by hostile outbursts, or in dealing with the sexual experiences of the individual, and as a result fail to show the necessary warmth and sympathy. Should these emotions emerge, self-examination by the priest is imperative. Self-directed questions such as the following will be found valuable. Is the parishioner I am dealing with doing anything to cause these emotions? Does the parishioner remind me of anyone I have known in the past, or am familiar with in the present? What do I feel about such a person as this parishioner with whom I am dealing? Do I anticipate that the parishioner will do anything disturbing whilst he is being interviewed? To arrive at the answers a great deal of self-explanation is necessary, but there will be a clearer indication of what projections may be at work.

The priest may feel bored—*Why?* He may consider the parishioner a hostile type of individual. His boredom may also be due to a defence which circumvents any hostility.

The priest may feel irritable—*Why?* He might have had similar feelings himself about a brother with whom he used to compete, and the parishioner resembles him in so many ways.

The priest may feel resentment—*Why?* The parishioner may talk about things which are stirring up resentful things in the mind of the priest.

When the priest is unable to resolve these disturbing emotions he should always refer his parishioner (or himself!) to another priest.

In order to help forward a good working relationship the priest can communicate an understanding of the problem. Every distressed soul wants the priest to be perceptive, competent, and to put into words his unspoken feelings. The priest must be sensitive to the moods and conflicts of those who consult him. He must show interest in the parishioner as a person, paying close attention to what the individual is saying. It is damaging to an effective working relationship to forget details which have been previously determined and mentioned. For this reason it is useful to make notes of all interviews and to keep records, but at the same time any impression of cross-examining must be avoided at all costs. (See suggested outline for notes at the end of this chapter.) Such notes prove most helpful to read before each successive interview.

The individual will often feel helpless, and will try hard to cover up inner turmoil. He looks upon his coming to the priest for help as an insignia of defeat. He will often expect a magical wiping away of all his troubles. The priest must control his own personal feelings, and communicate tolerance and acceptance. To counter-attack hostility with hostility is fatal. Equally damaging is the tendency to criticize the inability of the sufferer to think or express himself clearly. The priest should try to communicate objectivity, and this is assured by the tolerant, non-figurative manner in the face of any ideas expressed by the parishioner. He must remember that the present attitudes of the individual are not necessarily permanent ones, and that he has a right to his own opinions no matter how faulty he may feel them to be. It is not helpful to make him feel he is bowing to a superior being!

A relationship is always made secure where there is sympathy. All people have a desire to be liked, and a longing to be appreciated. How great is this desire among those in emotional or mental difficulty, for their neurotic problems make them feel unloved. Empathy conveys to them that their turmoil is understood, and that it is realized how upset they must be. As we have noted previously, it is the recognizing and the seeing things from their point of view. Warmth can be expressed by gestures and not only in words, and once the spirit of empathy is established there is considerable relief and sometimes an abatement of symptoms.

If our people are continually coming back to us for "refills" it may be an indication that something needs attention in our own personality set-up. In the past our distressed parishioners have probably gone to relatives, sympathetic friends, those with good judgement, and those who know a little about the valley of the shadow. This reveals the qualities that they look for in the office of the priesthood. We must love our people with an outgoing love which knows no stint—a love which is active outside as well as potent inside our own studies. We must seek a flexible mind with a growing spiritual experience. Izette de Forest reminds us again and again that the indispensable healing power in the therapeutic gift is love.

Love is the greatest force in influencing and transforming personality, for one can know another only through *agape*.

We must love the boring and the talkative as well as the interesting and the attractive. When this love is offered with openness and honesty, in the service of expert skill, it works as leaven—a leaven which lightens and effectively dissipates the burden of neurotic suffering and brings renewal of integrity and health. "The fundamental human problems do not lie in the region of the intellect", writes Guntrip. "They lie in the region of our personal needs and our emotional relationships, and they concern our basic satisfaction, fulfilments, and frustrations in living. We shall be closer to the heart of human problems if we think, not of 'guiding the perplexed', but of 'succouring the unloved'. What we need to know is how to remedy the ravages in human nature due to deprivation of love."[1]

PRACTICAL ISSUES

The priest should always make an appointment after the first visit rather than see people when they appear without warning. The very act of securing a specific appointment is reassuring and therapeutic. There must also be strictness about the time allotted, for when the parishioner sees time running out he will often present significant material. He should know that the interview is going to last thirty to forty-five minutes.

Do not counsel neurotic persons without the knowledge and consent of the doctor and/or the psychiatrist, and beware of being bogged down with chronic neurotics who will sap the valuable time of the priest. So many prefer a "post" to lean on, than to undergo the exercises of learning to walk again. Do not become entangled in prolonged analysis of a neurotic personality, but deal with the immediate situation in a manner that at least does no harm, and if possible promotes growth and stability. The priest is not trained to deal with deep neuroses, delusions of grandeur, or persecution. Such cases must always be referred to the psychiatrist. Remember probably no one is qualified for every possible

[1] H. J. S. Guntrip, *Mental Pain and the Cure of Souls*, p. 20.

counselling situation. "I do not love thee, Dr Fell; the reason why I cannot tell!" Never be afraid to hand over to another priest near at hand, and always be humble enough to say, "I don't know!" To a sensitive priest silences can be alarming, but they can be creative, even more creative than speech if carefully handled.

Pray regularly for those you help. The troubled anxious soul who seeks help will indeed prove the best test of our own spiritual lives. "Such as I have, give I thee" is an inexorable spiritual maxim. We cannot give what we do not possess. There will be no light in our study, if we have not dwelt in his light. "If one has prayed and prayed aright about the people one is called to help", wrote Pym, "prayed about them one by one, prayed for the spirit of understanding and adaptability in unexpected meetings, then one is likely to be spiritually sensitive to the needs of others."

We must not be in a hurry to look for quick results, but "bring forth fruit with patience". We must not feel that things should be going faster, that the parishioner is wasting valuable time, or that he is talking about irrelevant matters. He must be left to proceed at his own pace, believing that when he is ready he will deal with appropriate problems. People are a long time becoming what they are, and we ought not to expect sudden transformations, no matter how much we may sympathize with Sullivan when he exclaims: "If we could only be told that a patient's trouble arises at point A, that it can be defined as disease B, and that it can be relieved by remedy C, through the use of technique D, we should feel as if we were getting somewhere!"[1]

It is always wise to arrange for a second or more interviews, when after prayer we can come back fresh to the situation. Troubled souls are in acute emotional distress when they come to see us, and the gates of their unconscious are ajar. We must always be conscious of the work of grace in the soul, and keep our egotism firmly in check.

[1] H. S. Sullivan, *The Psychiatric Interview*, Introduction, p. xvii.

The priest must beware of falling into stereotyped ways of dealing with people. So often he will tend to think that every problem is just like another, and fail to recognize the uniqueness of each personality. If the priest makes the mistake of regarding a parishioner as just one of a group or type, rather than an individual, he will fail to understand why his particular problem is a problem to him. He must help each to become what God intended him to be, not to make him what he thinks he ought or would like to be, not to make him the self he thinks he is, or the world expects him to be. So many problems arise when people try to act out another role in life than their own.

Although a non-judgemental and non-condemning approach in counselling is sound psychologically, if the counsellor is a priest there must be exceptions. When a priest has to deal with a parishioner in a state of moral relapse or in acute anxiety, Pym advises that the counsellor assume responsibility and exert what force of will he can bear, and, if need be, all the authority of his office, to meet the situation —"Now you must do exactly as I say!" In these circumstances it is the duty of the priest to disapprove of opinions which he finds unacceptable, but he must be careful to distinguish between this attitude and the rejection of the person who holds them. He will condemn the error or sin without rejecting those involved.

If a right atmosphere has been fostered throughout the interview the parishioner will become honest and open about his feelings and thoughts. It is therefore not so much the counsellor who becomes non-judgemental, but rather the atmosphere and relationship.

The priest should not under normal circumstances agree or express opinions about what the parishioner has said, e.g. "My wife upsets the home everyday. She drinks heavily and I'm fed up. You can't blame me, can you?" "No, you've been very badly treated and your wife should know better!" Although it may be tempting, it is not helpful to relate one's own experiences, e.g. "Well, I've been through exactly the same thing you know, but everything turned out well in the end!"

Great harm can be done by "amateurs", who suggest quick and easy solutions, and "rules of living", before the vital and basic problems have been brought out into the open. The priest should never interview when he is tired, for it is so easy to take out his tiredness on the next person interviewed. He may diagnose correctly and say all the right things, and yet not help because he himself is below par.

Try to refrain from counselling someone who is so near you emotionally as to be involved in your life. It should always be remembered, too, that those who seek help in emotional distress sometimes feel embarrassed afterwards. They will think that they should not have said all they did, or that it was just silly or childish to act or feel the way they did. Consequently they may wish to avoid the priest for some little time afterwards. If the priest is aware of this danger he can often anticipate it by explaining to the person that this often happens.

Whether we sit in the chair of the helper or of the one being helped, we are all in the same human boat, and "it is this attitude of humble willingness to be taught as well as to teach; to be guided rather than to guide, which is the foundation of a loving therapy".[1]

In the last resort it is not what the priest does which is all important, but what he himself is in that moment which determines the result of his counselling. It is his personal faith, and his humble recognition of his own dependence upon the Holy Spirit which is the decisive factor, rather than any forms of technique. The priest must possess great sensitivity and a love for souls. Technique can certainly help, but far more than this the priest must rely on God's grace and mercy, and an honest criticism of himself. It is so true that "the first requirement in a shepherd of souls is that he should be a man of God. He cannot expect that knowledge of human

[1] Carol Murphy, *The Ministry of Counselling* (Pendle Hill Pamphlet).

nature or careful attention to technique are anything but second in importance to his own knowledge of God."[1] He must work, not in a dualism of counsellor and parishioner, but a trinity of Creator, parishioner, and priest. Unless he knows himself he will fail miserably in all his work with troubled and distressed souls, for he himself is the most effective tool he can have. "But by the grace of God I am what I am: and his grace which was bestowed upon me was not in vain; but I laboured more abundantly than they all: yet not I, but the grace of God which was with me." (1 Cor. 15. 10.)

[1] Pym, *Spiritual Direction*, p. 41.

NOTE TAKING

Dates of Interviews:	Full name
	Address: Tel. No:
	Age:
	Occupation:
	Family Background:
	Religious life and background:
	Names and addresses Doctors/Psychiatrists:
	Reports of above:
	Problem:
	Discussion Topic discussed: Report of Interview:
	Summary Needs of Parishioner: Meeting of Needs:

3

The Priest and Psychosomatic Disorders

The world is too much with us; late and soon,
Getting and spending, we lay waste our powers.

WORDSWORTH

Don't worry over anything whatever, tell God every detail of your needs in earnest and thankful prayer, and the
peace of God, which transcends human understanding,
will keep constant guard over your hearts and minds as
they rest in Christ Jesus.

Phil. 4, 6, 7 (J. B. Phillips' translation)

For as he thinketh in his heart, so is he.   Prov. 23. 7

Psychosomatic medicine attempts to bridge the hitherto
unbridgeable gulf between *mental cause* and *physical symptom*, for this medical approach recognizes a connection
between violent repressed rage, for example, and an attack
of lumbago, or between acute and prolonged anxiety and a
duodenal ulcer. Today many doctors are beginning to recognize that the real cure of many such conditions must involve
getting at the underlying psychological condition, e.g. the
anxiety, the fear, the resentment, etc. This is where modern
psychology joins hands with medicine, instead of, as formerly,
being dissociated from it, and where, therefore, modern
psychology forms a link between medicine and the Church's
ministry of healing.

If a person witnesses a bad street accident, for example, he
would rightly describe it as "a sickening sight", and indeed
might excusably be sick on the spot. This would be described
as a psychosomatic condition—Psyche (mind), Soma (body)

—the mind expressing its emotions through the body. The symptoms of sickness would not be those of indigestion or gastric ulcer, and the person would not expect to be treated by bismuth or stomach medicines. Our language is, indeed, full of expressive phrases which describe the effect of emotional activity upon the appearance and working of the body. One has only to recall such phrases as, "livid with anger", "he makes me sick", "one's hair stands on end", "cold feet", "jaundiced outlook", "pale with fright", etc. Whilst these expressions are regarded as figures of speech, they may well be described as "organ language".

Such complaints as migraine (sick headache), asthma, and skin disorders are often psychosomatic. Gastric and duodenal ulcers, diabetes, high blood pressure, and even rheumatoid arthritis can also be partly caused by worry, or the strain and stress of modern life—real organic diseases, in fact—which are almost entirely due to the disturbance of the emotional side of the human being. The treatment, obviously, becomes mainly psychological rather than medicinal and is aimed at restoring the patient's confidence by reassurance and suggestion, as well as the practices of our religious belief. In the consulting room the doctor finds that 75 per cent of the laboratory tests he does to check whether there is organic disease or not are negative. So his diagnostic tools become common sense and sympathy instead of a stethoscope; love and kindness instead of a clinical thermometer. He must learn to regard every patient as a very lovable human being in distress (dis-ease). Symptoms are never "mere imagination", but are very real indeed. It is just that the cause of those symptoms is emotional stress, rather than organic poisons or germs.

When we indulge in violent rage, or outbursts of anger, a number of internal changes takes place. When the sympathetic nervous system is stimulated, adrenalin pours into the blood. The output from the heart is increased and more blood is supplied to the brain and muscles. In resentment there is a slowing of the pulse, a weakening of heart action, and a drop in blood pressure. In hatred there is a rise in blood pressure, obstruction of the bronchial tubes, and a lowering of blood sugar. Digestive juices are put out at an abnormal rate. Chronic resentment brings about chronic changes which are the reverse of those found in fear and rage.

Before we outline some of the more common traits of personality observed in the field of psychosomatic medicine it is wise to heed the warning of Flanders Dunbar, who writes of the perils of "mistaken identity" in the following terms: "A mistake often made by those who are just beginning to understand the psychosomatic approach to themselves and others is that one or even five or six traits which are characteristic of certain disease types may be regarded wrongly as conclusive evidence of the existence or the threat of that disease. Quite a few people are fond of their mothers and have a desire to be independent. Not all of them are necessarily susceptible to ulcers. A lot of chubby, intelligent, ambitious fellows with sensitive natures and strict parents will never develop hypertension. It is the whole personality that matters, not its parts. . . . There is danger that an inexperienced layman might lop off a few limbs in the personality, never knowing that they were there, in order to fit himself or a friend into a supposedly healthy pattern of thought."[1]

The influence of the emotion on the respiratory system is well known. The sudden cessation of breathing in anxiety is often referred to as "breath-taking", or one says, "it took my breath away". Sighing is a common expression of despair. A stimulation of the para-sympathetic nervous system will cause the bronchial tubes to narrow. The aperture is decreased and so there is less air. Anything that increases the thickness of mucous membrane will decrease the bronchial tubes and make a person susceptible to *asthma*. Such a thickness may occur through infection. Frequent colds, too, restrict the bronchial tubes. Mucous membrane can also be inflamed

[1] Flanders Dunbar, *Mind and Body: Psychosomatic Medicine*, pp. 251 f.

through various pollens such as dust, or foreign proteins, e.g. hay fever. There are therefore two ways in which the respiratory system can be disordered. It can become so either through infection that thickens the mucous membrane, or through overstimulation of the nervous system. It is interesting to learn that asthmatics very rarely cry, and many will boast they have not cried for years. Those who refuse to cry may be wanting to cry far more than the rest of us and the asthmatic person is often found to "weep with his lungs instead of with his eyes". Some asthmatic attacks do seem to be almost a perverted form of having a good cry, and when under treatment, some of these deeper factors become clear to the patient, who often abandons asthma and cries his first tears for years.

There is good medical evidence to suggest that purely psychic stimuli may precipitate an attack. Any excitement will cause the chest to tighten. With others a particular emotional state will act as a precipitatory factor. Some researchers claim that particular situations, i.e. a separation from mother, or mother-substitute, will give rise to attacks. Often separation has psychological effects. The person does something which will offend mother or parents, and so is stricken with remorse, and the whole affair is repressed.

A young woman, over twenty-one, commenced asthmatic attacks when trying to break away from parental care and go out to dances. Her parents disapproved of such behaviour as unbecoming. They did not express their disapproval, but there was an air of reproof in their manner. The girl felt this bitterly. After some months of unaccustomed gaiety she was seized on the eve of a dance with an asthmatic attack, and for the next four years had regular attacks so timed as to prevent her from leaving her parental nest for any occasion of pleasure. She was not prevented from attending work at the office, and only had attacks when preparing to go off in the evenings to a dance or other social event. Her illness was in fact carrying out her father's unexpressed wish to subdue what he regarded as licentious activities. It was clear that the girl's conscience (*super-ego*) agreed with her father, and so although she ardently wished to enjoy herself, the prospect of a party or dance was accompanied by guilt feelings. A feeling of guilt was the precursor of attack.

A tension in the parent-child relationship does seem to be evident in many cases of asthma. It is not always guilt; it often is jealousy. Alexander points out that a very consistent find in his researches with asthmatic cases was the precipitation of an attack when the dependent relation with the mother was threatened. He says that *asthma nervosa* (a condition in which the chief factor is a nervous one) is the equivalent to a suppressed cry for the mother, suppressed mainly for fear of rejection. Very often, he goes on, he finds rejecting mothers in the histories of asthmatic patients.

Other researches have revealed three dominating factors in the personality pattern of asthmatic children. They had above average intelligence, but were aggressive with a marked irritability. Sometimes they suffered from a lack of self-confidence. Of the thirty children investigated ten were only children and six were only sons.

Tension appears to be the key factor, for the asthmatic has a personality which renders him particularly subject to tension. He tends to be fussed and overprotected, and although at first sight the parents may seem entirely at fault, we often find that the child himself does everything to encourage their misguided intentions. He is apt to revel in making them his slaves, for this satisfies his sense of insecurity, and to some extent his aggressiveness. But it also robs him of his freedom, and so brings him into an asthmatic-producing state of frustration and tension.

The observations made on a patient at Cornell University, U.S.A., by Wolf and Wolff[1] have brought many helpful points to light on the effect of the emotions on the *gastro-intestinal system*.

Tom was an assistant in the laboratory of the Clinic, and unfortunately swallowed some acid which burnt his oesophagus. He was unable to feed himself and an opening (a surgical fistula)

[1] S. Wolf and H. G. Wolff, *Human Gastric Function* (O.U.P.).

had to be made in the abdomen into his stomach. Observations were made for the behaviour of the stomach under different emotional states and the following are some of the findings. A normal condition showed that acid was being continuously secreted in small amounts. In fear or sadness the acid secretion became inhibited, and the mucous membrane as the blood concentration tended to decrease. When Tom was angry or resentful his stomach flow of acid increased. His mucous membrane flushed as blood concentrated itself and stomach contractions increased in frequency and vigour.

It has been said that the stomach is one of the most responsive organs in the body, for we know that it may react to almost every emotion and sensation that man is capable of experiencing. All these changes in the stomach resulting from anger or hostility make the mucous membrane liable to erosion and the stomach wall is left unprotected. The mucous membrane surrounds an organ for protection, and when the mucous membrane is flushed, then the organ is liable to attack. Haemorrhages can then occur even from the scratches of food particles, e.g. toast. Once they begin the wound is open to constant attack by the acid gastric juices and so a peptic ulcer is well on the way.

Although there is a great deal of agreement in the literature on this disorder in the psychosomatic field, the disagreement and speculation still make it most difficult to describe any clear-cut and accurate theories. The dominant factor seems to be worry. Little everyday problems seem to cause far more trouble than major ones, and the sufferer is inclined to take everything very seriously.

The normal treatment for ulcers is either surgical removal or rest, diet, and medication. Statistics reveal that 65 per cent of patients redevelop ulcers within two years of treatment, and a great number of the other 35 per cent have recurrences within five years. Gainsborough and Slater[1] in "A Study of Peptic Ulcer" in the *British Medical Journal* state that: "The results of medical treatment were disappointing and on our

[1] 24 August 1956.

figures one third of patients can be expected to relapse within four months. The failure was not as regards the healing of the ulcers, but in the prevention of relapses after return to work. Consequently more attention should be paid in the follow-up period to the adjustment of work conditions, the use of resettlement facilities under the Disabled Persons Act, and the careful discussion with the patient of his social and psychological problems."

It is interesting to note that under normal conditions all the lower animals never develop ulcers. The animal kingdom does not worry. It is also rare to find a negro with an ulcer, for as a race they are carefree and happy-go-lucky. A great majority of gastric disorders are generally found in people who have a strong unconscious longing to be given love and care. Because this is an unconscious state they are over-active and highly efficient people, and have a high standard of behaviour. They are always prepared to give out, support many causes, help many people, assume responsibilities, and if they are honest they will confess they enjoy having other people being dependent upon them. Yet all this seems to be a mask, covering an underlying desire to be helped themselves—in fact, a gnawing hunger for affection. It is very like the infant's desire to be cared for, loved, and fed by his mother. Such a repressed hunger was first associated with feed at his mother's breast where love and food were equated, and it serves as a constant stimulus to those cells which line the wall of the stomach, whether there is food present there or not. Under this constant stimulation the stomach behaves as it should only behave during digestion.

It is important to point out that not all such people have ulcers. A constitutional or acquired weakness of the stomach is important in the development of ulceration. It is the *whole personality* that matters, not its parts, for there are no two patients alike.

In the sacramental nature of man, disease is dis-ease—a state of unquiet. The burdens of the soul pass over to be served by the body. We may find in many forms of *rheumatism* outward signs of inward tensions provoked by external events or an accumulation of internal conflicts. The very symptoms, feeling sore or stiff, may be said to represent a person's deep-seated feelings of being hurt by circumstances, and resenting them in the sense of being "sore" about things and feeling them "stiff". When such feelings are expressed in an outward way, they are pushed out of the mind, so that the sufferer's attention is distracted from the problems of life, and becomes absorbed in his bodily feelings.

Psycho-analytical research has shown the importance in rheumatism of deep-seated feelings of resentment and hostility, and suggests that aggressiveness which is felt by the person towards another individual or situation, and which he is unable to express in appropriate muscular activity, turns inwards towards the person, who thus in one sense attacks and hurts himself. Complaints of pain and stiffness tend to arise in situations which provoke frustration, resentment, disappointment, bereavement, and loneliness. Often there are pains or stiffness experienced in the act of bending (neck, lumbar region, scapula), and these can sometimes be associated with primitive feelings (unconscious) of obstinacy, refusal, or unbending pride. There is a primitive archaic way in which we all express anger-negation. A baby before it is even able to talk says "no" to a toy or food offered it by throwing back its head, and extending its spine in rigid refusal!

Sometimes sufferers are found to be persons who live alone in a physical and perhaps also a psychological sense. They are cold, reserved, proud, and melancholy personalities. They never seem able to express themselves adequately to their fellows. "So often we find these patients wearing abdominal supports, when what they need is *inner* support. Instead of trying to bolster them up with a crutch, what we ought to do is to try to develop their inner emotional security so that they will not have to lean on supports or braces, or for that matter, on their physician."[1]

---

[1] E. Weiss and O. S. English, *Psychosomatic Medicine*, 2nd edit. p. 743.

It has been known for a long time that *rheumatoid arthritis* may recur as a response to some disturbance or life-situation. The illness is an outward manifestation of the total personality, and this self-restriction is an important factor pastorally for the priest. This condition is sometimes found in people with a predisposition to develop a particular physical and psychological pattern. When such a person encounters disturbing circumstances such as bereavement, he bottles up the emotional tension which arises. He hugs his grief and restrains his anger. This tension results in a disturbance of the autonomic and endocrine systems, which in turn leads on to a metabolic alteration in the person with this particular physical pattern. There results as an end-product his rheumatoid arthritis.

There appears, then, to be extreme emotional insecurity in the lives of many of those who are afflicted with this disorder. This is coupled with strong feelings of inadequacy and inferiority. The persons concerned seem to be in constant fear of rejection. They tend to avoid close relationships for fear of being dominated, and are often seen to be both physically and intellectually over-conscientious and over-active. Here again we see a strong connection with emotional stress.

The *skin* is the organ of repression, and the saying "the skin is the mirror of the mind" rings very true. As far as the personality pattern can be outlined, it appears to be one of shyness, reserve, over-sensitiveness, social anxiety, diffidence, and self-consciousness. Many skin sufferers are lonely people, and seem unable to form long and lasting friendships. Their illness is usually associated with a personal loss of some sort. They are inclined to be rather afraid of responsibility and blame everything apart from themselves for their condition. Dunbar describes the outstanding feature of the typical sufferer from skin disease as a deep-seated emotional conflict between desire for affection and a fear of being hurt if they seek it. "Touch me and comfort me", they seem to say in one breath, but "Don't touch me" in the next.[1] Scratching

[1] Dunbar, op. cit., p. 190.

seems to be of great etiological significance, for the important factor in scratching is the hostile impulse. This, on account guilt feelings, is deflected from its original target and is turned against one's own self. The following case-history illustrating guilt feelings in the skin disorder known as *urticaria* or nettle-rash is taken from *A Psychiatrist's Note-book*.[1]

A young woman of nineteen described repeated attacks of swelling of the skin of her arms and face which, she said, "came out of the blue". In addition to the rash she was irritable, slept badly, and had a twitch of one eyelid. During the exploration of the background of the *urticaria*, she was given a small amount of relaxant drug by injection, and asked to talk about her dreams. Discussion of these soon led to a confession. She ran away from home two years before to escape from an ailing and exacting mother, came to London and found herself a job. She was diligent and capable at her work, did well, and was promoted. The paradox was, however, that the more progress she made in her new life, the less happy she felt, for at the back of her mind she had a strong sense of guilt about having abandoned an ill parent. Every time something happened which aroused these guilt feelings, she had some swelling of the skin. It was not until she replanned her life, and arranged for her mother to be cared for, that she had relief.

To prepare for meeting emergencies, the body mobilizes glucose (energy producing) which makes the muscles react. There is exactly the same process and mobilization when there is a threat against security or prestige. Homeostasis or balance is maintained by the pancreas, which is the insulin producing organ, and which regulates the amount of sugar in the blood. Cannon (who coined the word "homeostatic" from the Greek "homois": like, similar; and "static": position, standing—hence the ability to remain the same) has shown that in fright, fear, anger, and worry, the amount of sugar in the blood is increased. To create homeostasis again,

[1] "The Stress of Life", *A Psychiatrist's Note-book* (*The Sunday Times*, June 1957), p. 12.

the pancreas carries an extra load to produce insulin. If the load is continuous and excessive, then invariably the pancreas becomes damaged and there is a shortage of insulin. The sugar in the blood has to be dealt with, and it goes through the kidneys into the urine.

The causes of *diabetes* are many and complicated and not all are emotional. In about one-third of the cases the significant factor appears to be hereditary. About 50 per cent have a history of trauma (shock), such as financial difficulty or death in a family which causes the person to assume more responsibility. There is often over-indulgence in food in order to overcome feelings of insecurity.

The personality profile is one of a person who is generally agreeable. He acts and looks younger than his years, but indecision and anxiety seem to stand out. Male diabetics especially seem unable to take the initiative in important matters and ask you to make decisions for them, and even then do not always act on them. Although they are people who like doing things for others, they will not do it unless others are socially inferior. In general, they give little and make very considerable demands. Research has revealed that in almost all cases there is a history of friction in their homes between parents, and often hatred towards one parent. A large number of diabetics seem dominated by their mother and prefer her to their father.

The marked characteristics of their behaviour pattern appear to be an inability to follow any consistent course of action, and probably more than any other disease group they consider that they are the victims of surroundings. They tend to postpone decisions and diffuse energy rather than direct it in any constructive line. Any situation which necessitates great responsibility readily becomes a focus of emotional turmoil, and this, coupled with indecisiveness, seems to keep them in painful situations and leads them to a life of "wear and tear".

What has the priest to contribute to these and many other psychosomatic disorders? Is he to stand by and wait for medicine to discover ways of easing stress through drugs of various sorts, or is he to meet the challenge of this age of tension, bringing the strained soul in utter faith and confidence to the love and peace of a personal God, and opening the way for bodily restoration. We shall proceed to discuss various methods by which this can be achieved, outlining first of all some of the main characteristics of stress.

PASTORAL CARE

In this field of medicine there have been great advances, but the picture as yet is still unsatisfactory. This is particularly true in the formation of any particular "personality type". Many such descriptions contain similar features, and off-hand it becomes quite impossible to indicate what disorder is referred to by the description of any one "personality type". What is important, however, for the priest is that the common factor in most of the psychosomatic states is that of emotional *stress* or *tension*.

Of late, much research has been carried out on its effect in psychosomatic disorders. Stress has been described by that great pioneer, Hans Selye (McGill University), as the "rate of wear and tear in the body". No one can escape stress, for without some stress we just could not exist. It is part of life and necessary for life. There are, however, different degrees and various forms of stress—mental, emotional, and physical. The most important factor is not the actual stress itself, but its effects. Seyle tells us that it is in understanding how to take stress, how to get stress to work for and not against, how to avoid excessive physical or mental stress, that the individual learns how to fight disease, and how to strengthen his bodily defences against "the wear and tear of life". The stress which plays havoc with us is the type that makes it difficult for us to relax, such as intense and persistent anger, frustration, fear, and anxiety.

In his introduction to Hans Selye's book on *The Stress of Life*, Sir Heneage Ogilvie describes the people he would put into the pigeon-hole of stress diseases. "They are", he writes, "between the ages of fourteen and forty. They have left the shelter of the home and are fighting their way through the world, but they have not yet reached success or given up the struggle as hopeless. They are normally engaged in work of the mind, involving decisions and the acceptance of responsibility, rather than in manual toil. They are intelligent, conscientious, and ambitious above the average, and single-minded in their determination to succeed. They have usually suffered some recent augmentation of the strain to which they are subjected, either the taking of some more difficult job that is proving rather too much for them, or the addition of some emotional stress—an engagement newly made or newly broken, a clash of personalities at work or the break up of a home. They are usually heavy cigarette smokers, but this may be an index rather than the cause of the mental stress. They may be men or women and the sex has some bearing on the form the breakdown takes. . . . What is the stress to which these people are exposed? It is not fear. It is not exhaustion —physical or mental. For want of a better definition it can be described as prolonged combat of uncertain outcome. The sufferers from the stress are constantly striving for something that seems to be attainable but that they do not succeed in attaining. They are constantly fighting, not a particular person, but 'them', a world that is trying to get them down or to keep them down."

In order to face stress courageously, the Christian is fortified by faith, prayer, and the sacraments. It is only in this context that he can find what Paul Tillich describes as *The Courage to Be*. As body and soul are so closely interrelated, the resistance of the body is strengthened by the fortitude of the soul.

In January 1954 *The Practitioner* devoted its whole number to a symposium on "Stress". In the editorial of this issue the medical reader was told that "the last word lies with the priest". It was also indicated to the doctor-reader that the Church has its answer as to how this stress can be eased, if not abolished, in the lovely old words of the Prayer Book, "The Peace of God, which passeth all understanding...." "Has medicine anything to offer", asks the Editor, "not as an alternative, but as an accessory? Perhaps, it is in the answer to this question that there lies the solution of the problem of stress as seen in this twentieth century of ours." Words from such a source have a poignancy of their own!

What then is the task of the priest when he ministers to those with psychosomatic disorders? They are, as we have seen, suffering from a mismanaged emotional life. Therefore their spiritual life is of the utmost importance, for a firm religious life is by far the best guarantee of a stable emotional life.

Working hand in hand with the general practitioner or the psychiatrist, the priest in his pastoral ministry will try to transform the sufferer from his tied-up state into a free and relaxed channel of God's grace. He can teach the sufferer that he was created in God's image, that he is a "child of God", and that his body is meant to be a perfect instrument for the expression of that wholeness (or holiness) of the Father. A mind purged of the negative emotional states by the power of Christ and filled with love, joy, and peace will radiate health rather than disease.

The priest should be aware of the danger of assuming that the familiar physical symptoms are unimportant. It is only the doctor who is competent to decide when real organic disease is evident, and a medical diagnosis should always be made before the priest undertakes his counselling. Symptoms of real disease can so easily be overlooked or mistakenly attributed to psychological causes.

Where repressed guilt is a causative factor, the confessional brings immense relief not only to the spiritual condition but also to the physical. For example, asthmatic sufferers find great relief when "they are able to confess, rather freely, episodes, thoughts, or desires which they have never dared mention before or which they thought they had forgotten. Confession, whose soothing effect has long been known in the religious world, seemed to have much the same effect upon the asthmatic as a fit of weeping".[1]

Short periods set apart for relaxation and meditation are of the utmost value for the deepening of the sense of communion with God. For such periods silence and quiet are essential. The psalmist (Ps. 46. 10) who advised his readers to "Be still, and know that I am God", realized this great need to be quiet. If this advice was needed two thousand years ago, we can well imagine how much more it is needed in the world of today, for so many people seem to suffer from a kind of psychic "St Vitus's Dance". So many cannot let go or relax, and are chronically keyed up. Pascal, the French philosopher, said that "all the evils of life have fallen upon us because man will not sit alone quietly in a room". More and more psychiatrists are realizing that religion is a means of letting go the strain, stresses, and tensions of life, and resigning oneself to an outside power. Indeed, one psychiatrist goes so far as to say that we all ought "to give our minds a mental bath each night before we go to sleep, and so try and erase from our minds all unkind thoughts, vengeful feelings, things unpleasant and disagreeable, and so sleep with a conscious void of offence towards God and men". Those who have learned to meditate and pray are in possession of the pearl of great price, whereby they are able to cast their care upon God, "knowing that he careth for us". They prove that "perfect love casts out fear".

Those are wise words of St Francis of Sales: "Do not lose your inward peace for anything whatsoever, even if your whole world seems upset. . . . Commend all to God, and then lie still and be at rest on His bosom . . . and if you find you have wandered forth from this shelter, recall your heart quietly and simply. . . . Examine yourself often as to whether your soul is 'in your hand', or whether it has been wrested thence by any passionate or anxious emotion. . . ."

St John of the Cross knew of the great value of such silence: "Learn to abide with attention in loving waiting upon God

---

[1] Dunbar, op. cit., p. 111.

in the state of quiet ... the more the soul is disposed to tranquillity, the more will it grow therein, and the more conscious it will be of loving knowledge of God which brings peace and rest and sweetness and delight without trouble."

Gladstone was once asked how he managed to keep serene and composed in the midst of so hectic and busy a life. He replied: "At the foot of my bed, where I can see it on retiring and on arising in the morning, are the words, 'Thou wilt keep him in perfect peace whose mind is stayed on Thee'."

A consultant physician, speaking at a meeting of doctors and clergy,[1] had this to say about the great value of meditation: "I cannot overstate the importance of the habit of quiet meditation for health of body, mind and spirit. Modern man's life is grossly abnormal. Our days are spent in continuous activity and our senses stimulated incessantly, so that we have neither time nor opportunity for quiet. We search for the Kingdom of Heaven in every quarter except where we are told on excellent authority that it happens to be—*within* us. We need to meditate daily on great truths. We need to explore our own lives, motives, our plans, in the clear light God provides as we sit quietly and unhurriedly in His presence. ... It is imperative that modern man should cultivate this God-directed quietness. It is the only firm foundation for serenity, for the quiet mind. ... In my view the main single factor which leads to 'wholeness' is a vital and valid religious experience based on moral standards and refreshed by disciplined daily meditation. ... By 'meditation' I do not mean 'dreaming on religious themes'. Meditation presupposes a classification of thought and feeling. In the ultimate, it is the expectant waiting upon God's Will of a man whose self-will is broken. ..."

[1] "A Prescription for Health", lecture by Dr R. W. Luxton, Consultant Physician at Crumpsall Hospital and the Christie Hospital and Holt Radium Institute, Manchester, at a Meeting of Doctors and Clergy held at Newcastle-on-Tyne, July 1957. This lecture, together with another by the Right Reverend A. S. Reeve, Lord Bishop of Lichfield, is published in a booklet entitled *A Prescription for Health*, Churches' Council of Healing.

Dr J. L. Halliday, an authority on psychosomatic medicine, has formulated various causes of illness. He feels that illness should be regarded under three fields of observation:

1. The field of the *person*. Under this heading would be considered the various characteristics of the person before he became ill. In this field the question is asked: *"What kind of person was this?"*

2. The field of the *environment*. Here is examined the various factors of environment which the person experienced at the time of falling ill. The question arises: *"Why did he become ill when he did?"*

3. The field of *mechanism*. Here are observed the various characteristics which ultimately brought about the particular mode of behaviour, and so the question is asked: *Why did he become ill in the way he did?"*

Here is a field of practical co-operation between priest and doctor, for who better than the parish priest, who knows his people, to answer some of these questions. He knows the many problems and stresses of his parochial families, and it is he who visits them in their environment and observes their background. Both, therefore, assist in the recovery of the psychosomatic sufferer.

Some of the most famous pioneers in emotional and psychosomatic disorders themselves testify to the great therapeutic value of a religious outlook on life. Weiss and English in their standard work on *Psychosomatic Medicine* state that: "It is the childish parts of the personality which are in great need of love and reassurance in illness of emotional origin. Hence, when conflicts produced by guilt, hostility, and sexuality produce pain and suffering, contact with a religious force may do much to bring relief".[1]

"You must find something to put in the place of worrying thoughts to chase them away," writes Selye, "and nothing erases unpleasant thoughts more effectively than conscious concentration on pleasant ones. Mental tensions, frustrations,

---

[1] Weiss and English, op. cit., p. 198.

the sense of insecurity, and aimlessness are among the most important stressors. As psychosomatic studies have shown they are also very common causes of physical disease. . . . How often are migraine, headache, gastric and duodenal ulcer, coronary thrombosis, arthritis, hypertension, insanity, suicide, or just hopeless unhappiness actually caused by the failure to find a satisfactory guide for conduct?"[1]

It is only by deep spiritual experience that we can be strengthened with might through his Spirit in the inner man, and thereby maintain a mature and whole personality.

[1] Hans Selye, The Stress of Life, p. 299.

4

The Priest and the Neuroses

Our souls are restless, O God, until they find their rest in thee.

ST AUGUSTINE

Thou wilt keep him in perfect peace whose mind is stayed on thee.

Isa. 26. 3

Though I am sometimes afraid yet put I my trust in thee.

Ps. 56. 3

There is a difference between psychiatry and other medical disciplines in that the mentally ill do not fit into neat diagnostic departments with any degree of accuracy. The psychiatrist cannot gain the security of the physician who labels the patient as having pneumonia or appendicitis, for there is no clearly marked dividing line between the normal, the neurotic, and the psychotic reactions. Normal reactions shade into the neurotic, and the neurotic into the psychotic. It is conceivable, consequently, that what is thought to be abnormal by one, may be considered within the range of the normal by another.

There is a marked distinction, however, between the well-developed psychoses and the neuroses. In the latter state there is a change affecting only a part of the personality. In the former the whole of the personality is changed. Before we proceed to discuss the various neurotic states, it may be helpful to outline the main "mental" or "defence" mechanisms, for these play a prominent and persistent part in both the neuroses and psychoses. It is therefore important for the priest to have some understanding of them, both in himself and in the persons with whom he deals.

From childhood onwards the ego builds up a series of so-called "mechanisms of defence". By means of these defences it attempts to deal with instincts whose gratification would be dangerous or painful for one reason or another. These mechanisms become more or less characteristic of the individual, and while he may use others, these are the ones which we may expect him to use in meeting the majority of his conflicts. It is not easy to draw a hard and distinct line between these various mechanisms, for one usually sees a combination of three or four utilized by one individual in confronting his problems. The priest must realize that they operate on an unconscious or more or less automatic level, so that the individual concerned is unaware of their existence or scope.

Sublimation is the only defence mechanism which can be considered to be well within the confines of normality. It requires a change in either the aim or the object of an instinct and then subsequent gratification. The other mechanisms as we shall see meet the instinct head-on, and so prevent its discharge. In this mechanism the instinct is turned into a new but useful and more acceptable channel. For example, an unmarried woman may find an outlet for her frustrated feelings of love and tenderness by caring for the sick, or teaching children.

Although the remainder of the defence mechanisms are found to some degree in every person, they can properly be labelled "pathological". They cannot be termed normal, in spite of their widespread occurrence, because of the inefficient way in which they operate. The ego is forced to allot a certain amount of energy in order to maintain these defences, and therefore it is not available for other and more constructive purposes.

Repression is an unconsciously purposeful forgetting of either internal urgings or external events, which, if they were to become conscious, would be painful or hurtful. This defence mechanism was the first to be described by Freud, and it formed the cornerstone of some of his earliest theories of psycho-analysis. The ego exerts sufficient energy against the objectionable memory, i.e. affect or instinct, to prevent its reaching consciousness. The simplest examples of repression are described by Freud in his *Psychopathology of Everyday Life*, where he discusses the forgetting of names and dates, and slips of the tongue. It may be that the name in question is of an individual whom one dislikes, or there may be some particular type of association between that name and an objectionable affect or idea.

By means of *projection* painful or objectionable affects or ideas are projected outward upon persons or things in the environment, and felt by the individual as belonging outside of himself. We often blame our personal shortcomings and failures on bad luck, or unfavourable material. More complex examples of projection are seen in the paranoid schizophrenic, in the form of hallucinations. He hears voices coming from the environment which accuse him of various things, which are present in his unconscious.

It is of immense importance to keep this mechanism in the forefront of our minds in giving spiritual counsel and hearing confessions, for no mental mechanism is of more importance to our healing work and ministry. We must always be on our guard lest we try to solve our own problem in those we attempt to help. Only constant awareness of this projection, and growing self-knowledge can be a real safeguard.

Denial is a defence mechanism whereby obvious reality factors are treated by the individual as if they did not exist. He probably finds certain factors unpleasant or painful and he literally denies they are present. When used excessively this mechanism is representative of a psychotic state of mind. One form of denial is the fantasy life, but this is relatively harmless if it does not interfere with the individual's task in the real world. It is important for the priest to realize that this mechanism, like the others, operates on an unconscious level, and therefore should not be confused with the conscious process of deliberate prevarication.

Introjection is a turning into the person of feelings and

attitudes towards others which give rise to conflict and aggressive impulses. It is often used by an individual either to acquire some trait or characteristic which is considered advantageous, or to destroy something which is considered dangerous. The depressed patient will often show a pathological example of this mechanism. The depressive frequently has a powerful undercurrent of hate towards persons he loves. When he feels rejected by such a person, he literally introjects him, and becomes the recipient himself of all the hate he previously held towards that person.

Regression is a mechanism by which the ego returns to an earlier and more infantile level. Sometimes the adult regresses to childish petulance and temper tantrums. Some individuals never seem able to outgrow earlier and infantile phases because the needs of those phases have never been met.

The schizophrenic patient is the most pathological example of regression, for his behaviour is often on an entirely infantile level. There is also a certain amount of regression in the neurotic person in that he has not really achieved a mature level of adjustment and behaves in some respects on an immature and unrealistic level.

Most of us use *rationalization* to distort facts to suit ourselves. Such a procedure is the reverse of logic, sincerity, and common sense, and yet its whole object is to convince ourselves first, and then others, that these are the very qualities which govern our thought and conduct. The very idea that we commit any action which we cannot explain to our satisfaction is intolerable, and hardly ever does the average adult find himself at a loss for some rationalization of some sort. The priest must always be careful to suspect that what the parishioner tells him is the cause of his condition may be, and probably is, rationalization.

By means of *displacement* an effect which was originally attached to one object is displaced to another, thus preventing a painful situation from developing. Affect which cannot find a proper object goes to and fro in the conscious mind to seek a substitute to which it can attach itself. It is not particular, for anything will do. The man returns from the office, chides the children, and kicks the cat. He is not really angry with either, but his chief has been overbearing all day at work! We all know mornings when everything seems to go wrong, and an explosion is only a matter of time. Anything seems to serve as a detonator!

The average person uses many defences in his attempts to meet his instincts and environment. When they become exaggerated he may either retire shyly from the environment, or meet it in an exaggerated aggressive way. A considerable amount of psychic energy is needed to keep these defences in operation, and we soon sense an artificiality in his behaviour.

CLASSIFICATION OF THE NEUROSES

Horney classified the neuroses according to their typical behaviour, either of "moving *towards* people, moving *against* people, or moving *away from* people", as a defence against basic anxiety.

The first type throws himself on the mercy of the priest or psychiatrist, often without much readiness for co-operation, and with all the claims and titles of infantile dependency. These people seem to have their centre of gravity outside themselves. They overvalue affection, not so much the affection they give, but the affection they receive and which they so greatly need for their own security. The tendency of these people is to please and placate everybody. They are masters in compliance, but also masters of manipulating others to serve their own interests. They are inclined to belittle themselves, and to appeal to sympathy. Many often seem masochistic, martyr-like, self-effacing, modest, and humble. They are very vulnerable and deeply offended when their manipulation does not work. They are flooded by anxiety when a situation really demands resourcefulness and self-assertion.

The second type is the neurotic who moves against people, who defends himself against anxiety by attacks on others, by aggressiveness and domination. This type has to be in control of a situation. He is extremely efficient, but restlessly active, over-tense, and frequently argumentative and conceited. He maintains the philosophy of the jungle—everybody is at everyone else's throat. What this neurotic type has dissociated is warmth, tenderness, and friendliness. His over-independence conceals his repressed dependency needs. He has not learned to reach out for others, and is ashamed of gentle feelings.

The third type defends himself against anxiety by withdrawal and detachment. He clings to the ideal of self-sufficiency, of not needing his fellow creatures. On the surface he may get along with other people very well, but he keeps them at arm's length. He does not get them involved, either in hatred or in love. He has squelched his emotions. He has an intensive fantasy life. Often ideas of grandeur have to make up for the emptiness of his real existence. His isolated perfectionism has to comfort him for his lack of close companionship, but he does not experience a belonging to others.

Sullivan also has outlined the various syndromes which demand psychiatric help, and in his classification the first group shows an arrested development all through their life career, while the second group also displays an arrested development which leads to acute disorders in inter-personal adjustment. In the first group we find the *self-absorbed persons*. Most frequently they develop disturbances of an hysteria nature. The self-absorbed person is frequently a persistent daydreamer who does not come down to earth. He avoids painful, frustrating experiences with what Charcot called "la belle indifférence des hystéries"—the beautiful indifference of the hysteric. Pain and frustration do not touch him.

The self-absorbed person is seen to be dramatic and exaggerated in his behaviour. He loves to talk in superlatives and reaches out for others, not so much to come to a mutual adjustment, as to use them as a source of comfort, security, and gratification. His tendency to falsify reality keeps him mainly at the receiving end in inter-personal relations. He is apt to ignore and overlook the needs of the other person. If anxieties are stirred up by external difficulties, the self-absorbed person evades them easily by flight into illness. The attention is fixed on the acceleration of the heart, the nausea, or indigestion, or whatever the autonomic disorder may be, and physical symptoms throw a complete blanket over the psychological conflict. The ailment takes the centre of attention, and becomes a device to demand the submission of others to the need of the patient. His adjustment to others is all sweetness and light, as long as there is no trouble or frustration. If the self-absorbed person cannot have his own way, panic looms up, and the characteristic hysteric evasion mechanisms come into action.

The *incorrigible person* shows different evasion, which stems from the hopelessness of gaining parental approval. This original hopelessness makes impossible the later submission to any authority, which for one reason or another can be blamed or attacked. The incorrigible person is compelled to find fault with others, because his own self-esteem can only be maintained if he can criticize and correct others. He may get along in a condescending fashion with other people whom he considers his inferiors, but he avoids competition and feels incapable of making compromise concessions to others. The inter-personal relations remain therefore one-sided, for there is no give-and-take possible. The incorrigible person is not at the receiving end like the self-absorbed person, but he is defending himself against rejection and disapproval by rejecting and disapproving first. This makes him intolerant and frequently quite intolerable to others.

The *negativistic person* has also had an overdose of disapproval in his infantile development, but he has developed a certain self-esteem out of his reactions of defiance, by which he has gained attention in childhood. It may be that an anxious, insecure mother submitted to his temper tantrums, or that for some other reason he has established the belief that by being difficult or resisting authority one can gain importance and power. Positive aspects of tender co-operation are more or less dissociated or repressed. He prides himself on not needing affection, and he prefers to be feared rather than loved. He often develops a high degree of competence and self-sufficiency, and in that way he may establish security and self-respect, but his psychological equilibrium is rather artificial and does not lend itself to a satisfactory integration with others.

The above-mentioned types of chronic personality disorder —the self-absorbed, the incorrigible, and the negativistic personality—are the result of an arrest of emotional development in the early periods of life, and show failures in co-operation and integration between parent and child. They become evident in the formative years before the child leaves the family circle. Other chronic personality disorders become evident in the later juvenile, preadolescent and adolescent phase, though their roots reach back into early childhood.

In the juvenile phase we frequently observe the development of *ambition-ridden characters*. These are the youngsters who can only establish security and self-respect if they win. They *have* to succeed. They cannot afford to fail, to share with others, or to be average, because that would endanger their self-respect, so they develop devices that guarantee success. They are either unscrupulous in the pursuit of success, or they develop clever devices to avoid competition, if victory is not absolutely sure. The preoccupation with ambition as a primary form of satisfaction prevents the ambition-ridden juvenile from developing any acquaintance with the satisfactions of comradeship. Inter-personal relations are submitted to the condition that they have to provide gratification of ambition. If this is not forthcoming, the relation is destroyed by envy which causes unbearable anxieties.

The *asocial characters* also emerge in the juvenile era. They are different from the incorrigible and negativistic persons in that they do not clash with others in any ostensible ways. They simply withdraw into their shells and are unobtrusive. Due to early lack of tenderness they do not have the confidence that they can be loved. They have developed a rather resigned attitude. The lack of *rapport* with others makes them rather dull and unstimulating. They are quite hopeless in establishing intimacy. But they get along on rather superficial contacts. The asocial person suffers mostly from his loneliness, but in a resigned fashion, for he is so used to his self-limitation that he seldom feels urged to make any revolutionary break with his habitual adjustment patterns.

Another type of fundamentally discouraged juvenile, whom Sullivan has named the *inadequate person*, establishes a precarious form of self-respect by becoming a satellite to presumably important people, by devotion to a cause, or by hanging on to some person or group, without developing his own personality. This method of avoiding anxiety is frequent in children of dominant parents who have been drilled into over-obedience. The spark of creativity and originality has been repressed too successfully. This adjustment pattern of the clinging vine may be a lifelong persistence, unless an involuntary break opens up new avenues of development. If the adjustment of inadequacy is maintained its dissatisfactions may easily find expression in chronic invalidism.

Immaturity stemming from various sources of retarded development creates the picture of the *chronic adolescent*. This is the person who is not able to establish a satisfactory heterosexual adjustment. He or she engages in more or less promiscuous behaviour, or withdraws completely into celibacy. The "eternal adolescent" seems to pursue an unattainable ideal. He does not come down to earth and settle, because the maintenance of unattainable ideals seems to be indispensable for his equilibrium.

These types of chronic personality disorder do not frequently seek the help of a psychiatrist. The persons concerned do not consider that there is anything wrong with them for they are so accustomed to their habitual adjustment patterns. They are more likely to seek psychiatric help if for some reason or another the self-system breaks down and the person is suddenly confronted with unmanageable anxieties.

A true state of *anxiety neurosis* is reached when anxiety becomes chronic and interferes with many of the pleasures of ordinary living, decreasing working ability and efficiency. The most frequent fears are those of death and insanity, and these are accompanied by an inability to concentrate. This state can often be the forerunner of a psychotic condition.

The priest must be able to distinguish between the salient features of *fear* and *anxiety*. Fear is always caused by something definite; anxiety is vague. Fear is the tendency not to fight against the danger, but to escape through flight. Anxiety has a far more destructive force, due to its indistinctness and haziness, for it knows no clearly recognized object and so creates tension and constriction (cf. Latin derivation, *Angus* —narrow). In anxiety one is in a state of being exposed to a situation with which one is unable to cope.

Mr Joseph F aged thirty-six years has been married for ten years, and has one child, aged four years. Mr F's father had been strict and rigid. He was the only boy in a family of five children, and the youngest child. His mother tended to over-compensate for the father's strict discipline. His father was an engineer's clerk, and had been rather disappointed at his son's achievements. One grandparent died many years ago of pulmonary tuberculosis. Mr F is an electrician, and most conscientious in his work. At present he complains of "panic" attacks, "tightness" in the chest, and says, "I cannot get my breath". He states that he worries because he is "not very strong" (in actual fact Mr F is six feet tall, and very well built). He worries in case he may make a mistake when doing his work. "I may electrocute some child if I connect my wires wrongly." He complains that his wife is cold, and disinterested in him, and that his married life has not been complete for some time now. He shows a lack of affection for the child.

Mr F always appears somewhat depressed, anxious, and tense. He finds he is unable to concentrate for any length of time, and is becoming more and more incapacitated as far as his electrician's work is concerned. He continues to worry about his physical health. "My grandfather had T.B., and my heart pounds at times."

This person shows typical anxiety symptoms. He is a somewhat inadequate type of personality, and worries very easily.

He has now transferred these worries on to his physical symptoms which are really only secondary to the anxiety state.

The *obsessional states* imply a variety of bodily ailments often of quite serious nature. However, these physical ailments are not used in inter-personal relations to gain sympathy in the way in which the hysteric or the self-absorbed patient does. The physical ailments of the obsessional are either of a cardio-vascular nature, or present chronic tension states of the digestive tract, gastric ulceration, etc.

The obsessional patient is mostly a very disciplined and controlled person. He is inclined to maintain his security by obscure power operations of a magical nature. These "magic power" operations can be traced back to early periods in the process of his development, in which as a child he lost confidence in parental guidance. He has therefore tried to gain security by his own perfection, omniscience, and omnipotence. Grandiose fantasies protect him against the anxiety of desertion and loneliness. Take for example the child who, by avoiding all the cracks in the pavement, holds his own fate or that of his family in his hands. He has a bomb-proof shelter against anxiety in such magic thoughts, gestures, or habit formations which, because of their function to ward off infantile anxieties, have to be carefully and meticulously maintained, and are not accessible to reasonable change. So we find the adult obsessional enmeshed in a system of cautions which do not make any sense. Here we find rituals, e.g. handwashing, ceremonials, and thoughts, the origin of which cannot easily be traced because their function as a defence against anxiety would be revealed.

An obsessional disorder frequently begins with a phobia or morbid fear, e.g. the fear of fainting or of losing one's mind. These phobias are intense and paralysing, despite the fact that the individual may realize that there is no rational basis for such fears. Notwithstanding this realization, the patient has very little control over them. The most well-known phobias include the fear of closed places (claustrophobia), the fear of high places (acrophobia), and the fear of open places (agoraphobia).

Mr Fred J is thirty-two years of age, and might be described as a rather wearisome person. He is inclined to be a "perfectionist". Nothing significant appeared in his past history, except that he was often afraid to go to sleep as a child, in case he should die. He used to bite his nails until well into his 'teens. All through life he wanted "to be something", and both at school and college he did rather well.

In his present condition he says, "I like to wash my hands many times a day", in order to get them "good and clean"! His wife states that he used to wash his hands for fifteen minutes, and stop the tap with his elbow. She also relates that after washing his hands he will not touch the door-knob, and on one occasion came in through the window to avoid touching the door handle. Apparently he explained his behaviour in the following terms: "I thought if I rubbed my hands a hundred times it would be all right, and then I wasn't sure if it was a hundred, and I would have to go back." He says he feels "uneasy" and "doubtful" about his confessions: "I don't seem to have enough sorrow for my sins."

Here we see an obsessive-compulsive reaction, the line being drawn between what might be normal by the fact that the person's life is being disturbed and thrown out of gear. In psychotic obsessive thinking the person struggles *with* his obsessions. In neurotic obsessive thinking he struggles *against* his obsessions.

One of the oldest of the known mental abnormalities is hysterics, and this term is now used to cover a particularly wide range of phenomena, from the hysterical fits of laughing and crying, to the complex disorders of multiple personality.

In many instances the hysteric adopts certain attitudes, usually bodily illnesses, in order to attain some end. He represents his inner psychological conflict by means of symbolic somatic disturbances. This condition is known as *conversion hysteria*. In this condition there are motor symptoms, which often involve the voluntary muscles of the body, and most characteristically, an extremity—a paralysis of one or of both legs or arms. Frequently this arises from a stress situation in which he wants to take a certain course of action and yet feels prohibition against the action. There are also sensory disturbances and these involve one of the special senses, e.g. blindness, deafness. It must be stressed that the symptom is produced through the unconscious of the person, and so he is not aware of its true meaning.

There is unfortunately a certain amount of stigma attached to "hysteria", and many will pass it off as "just mere imagination". Probably this is due to the fact that the person concerned has failed to adapt himself to the demands and responsibilities of life. However, he is in no way to blame for this state, for hysteria is most often due to predisposing causes in infancy over which he has little or no control.

A young man in show business joined the Army. He found the discipline rigid and the duties irksome. He longed for travel, excitement, and attention, and was most eager to return to civilian life again. To leave the Armed Forces would mean desertion. Suddenly he became paralysed and was quite unable to walk. Both his legs seemed insensitive to pain. Throughout this time he displayed a significant attitude of unconcern. The conflict of mind, instead of being consciously experienced, is "converted" into functional symptoms in organs or parts of the body enervated or supplied with sensory and motor nerves.

In the above example we see two conflicting motives at work. This young man could either conform to the rigid regulations of military life, or he could escape from a hated situation. At the same time there is a strong desire to maintain his self-respect.

The *hypochondriacal* personality is different from that of the hysterical in that the degree of self-centredness in the hypochondriacal person is even greater. He is much less eager to gain sympathy and support. With a certain fanatic glee he talks about his ailments, even when he is quite aware that he makes a nuisance of himself. There is more of the defiance which does not care what the other person feels or thinks. The priest will soon gain the impression that the hypochondriac person cannot live without his imaginary ailments for they form the basis of his pride and self-esteem, and he has to force others to listen to his tale of woe.

We find the same thing in certain *masochistic* personalities. They are not happy if they cannot complain about some misfortune. They find a pride in stressing the seamy side of life. They boast of their disasters and are quickly offended if one does not take their suffering seriously enough. It is very difficult to treat this habit of wallowing in misery, for the self-system clings to misery as a source of self-esteem and defence against anxiety.

PASTORAL CARE

As has already been stated, much will depend upon the training and the experience of the priest as to how far he can profitably and helpfully progress in the exercise of his pastoral care of the mentally ill. The beginner will naturally need to be very cautious and work under strict supervision of a more knowledgeable partner. Those who are experienced in depth psychology and the dynamics of personality disorders will obviously avoid the dangers of taking symptoms at their face value. Co-operation with the various professions working in the whole field of mental health will in any case be most essential. The following elements of pastoral care are offered to the priest or minister who is seeking practical help and guidance in his dealing with the emotionally disturbed, and their cautionary note only seeks to emphasize the danger of the over-confident and the irreparable harm that can be caused by the well-meaning amateur. Such a warning was given by the Archbishop of Canterbury in his presidential address to the Institute of Religion and Medicine, at the Royal Society of Medicine, June 1965:

> What disturbs me is the emergence of an undefined semi-trained category, where we have clergymen with a ready use of psychological jargon, a little knowledge, insufficient awareness of the pitfalls, and the supposition that they know a great deal more

than they really do know. If we could eliminate that category and be sure of the elementary training for all to show me how little I know, and the really thorough training for some, then I think we would have an objective to work to.

Our ministry to the neurotic personality calls for patience, understanding, and a sound religious experience. There will be no room for arrogance and self-righteousness, but a true sense of humility. The neurotic patient must be met with a mixture of sympathy and challenge, and the priest must be calm, full of assurance, modest, and "unshockable". Pastoral care is partly composed of listening, and giving the individual opportunity to revaluate the business of living. We must transmit hope, faith, and joy in living, helping the sufferer to build up a right reaction to life, with its pleasures and its problems. Our approach will therefore be positive rather than negative, for the mentally ill need something that will take possession of themselves and give meaning to their lives.

The attitude of the priest must be one of love. This is, of course, true of his attitude to all parishioners, but it must be especially so when dealing with the mentally sick. It was Menninger who said: "Love is the medicine for the sickness of the world, a prescription often given, too rarely taken. . . . If we can love, this is the touchstone, this is the key to all the therapeutic programmes of the modern psychiatric hospital. . . ."

It is not the priest's responsibility to analyse the disorder, and under no circumstances must he imitate the psychiatrist. He has neither the aptitude nor the training to try to become an "ecclesiastical psychiatrist". In the whole of his pastoral care of the mentally distressed, the priest, in his eagerness and enthusiasm to help, must ever be mindful of the grave danger of making religion just another of the therapeutic treatments. Naturally the priest will be interested in the recovery of the patient and do all he possibly can to further such progress, but he must not lose his priestcraft in the midst of a psychiatric atmosphere. This perhaps applies even more so to those priests who serve as full-time mental hospital chaplains. His whole approach should be easy and natural, leading the individual back to the sacraments where he may have lapsed and to prayer which he may have neglected. He should see the neurotic as a person, not in the sense that he is odd or abnormal, or even too much different from himself, for when he looks at the patient, he looks at himself, and when he works with the patient, he works with himself. We are all part of human society, a part of its ills and a part of its health.

So many of our people will need the assurance that neurosis is not something to be ashamed about. The patient often feels defeated and frustrated by the statement from the doctor that his difficulty is psychogenic. He would much prefer a physical or organic disorder. Why is this? It seems to him less shameful to succumb to an invasion of micro-organisms, for that is a defeat in the battle with nature. But, if a psychogenic disorder is diagnosed, then the patient is more or less aware that he is defeated in the battle with his fellow creatures. This realization endangers his self-respect far more than would an organic illness and he feels more insecure about the respect and the sympathy of his fellows. But we are all neurotic somewhere, and the sufferer is not inferior, less desirable, or to be pitied and avoided. He is so apt to look upon himself as an outcast, a lonely and misunderstood soul, and among his greatest fears is that of not being taken seriously.

Strictly speaking there is no such thing as a "nervous breakdown", and this popular term can be most misleading. The priest can point out most helpfully that a neurosis is not "just one of those things". It is usually accompanied by warning signs easily discernible to those who are trained in such matters. There is also the common misunderstanding that it is due to the result of overstrain and overwork. These are more often than not symptoms rather than causes. What is far more important to ask is: "Why did this person allow himself to be driven, or even drive himself, beyond all reasonable expectations?" Described very simply a neurosis is often a surface manifestation of a deep emotional difficulty. The various emotions often conflict with each other or with accepted standards. These emotional conflicts must eventually find an outlet. Generally speaking, the longer their expression or outlet is delayed, the more violent and unreasonable will it be when it can and does come out.

Self-knowledge is so very important in our dealing with afflicted souls. If the person can be shown that his neurosis has a purpose, that it is trying to achieve something, he gains courage to face his problems. "You may think that you know what the cause of the symptoms is, and you may tell him why he has become like that, and he may understand what you say. But that will not benefit him. Instead of getting better, he may sometimes get worse under such treatment, so that external knowledge of the cause of his illness is not sufficient for him. Self-knowledge is what he needs—a direct awareness."[1] The priest, by his love and compassion and understanding can then open up a way of recovery and growth, which may well lead on to healing. Like Job's comforters, many of the sick man's friends will have probably told him to "snap out of it", "pull yourself together", "buck up, old man!", "have faith, and you'll be all right".

The Christian religion has unrivalled treasures and resources. It provides a faith in a God who cares, giving the neurotic an assurance of a power beyond himself. There is the reality of forgiveness and the eternal significance of life. The answer of the priest therefore to the problem of neurosis lies in that peace in oneself which can only come from God.

It is the priest's task to deepen the religious convictions of the individual so that he may be brought to realize the real significance of life. Throughout his pastoral care he must not be forgetful of the many lessons that he himself can learn from those who are mentally ill. The Reverend Ernest Bruder, Chaplain of St Elizabeth's Hospital, Washington, D.C., has wise words to say in this respect:

As we come to know them and let them be our teachers, and hear from them something of the hurt they have encountered as

[1] William Brown, *Science and Personality*, p. 139.

they sought to become sons and daughters of God, then we may be able to gain something for which we are all striving. To be able to bear the anxieties of hearing of another's loneliness, or of the feelings associated with longings which are regarded as unacceptable, or of the estrangement which is so much part of our humanness, or of the anger and bitter resentment that can well up when he cannot reach or be reached by another, or of the tenderness deep within, which often terrifies because we are afraid of the ways in which it seeks to be expressed—these are priceless gains which we seldom can achieve unless we have been helped to sit at the feet of those who are most troubled by them.[1]

ANXIETY AND EXHAUSTION STATES

The priest will find that in these states present-day relationships are often distorted. There are signs of an inhibited life due to anxiety and preoccupation with oneself. To one so afflicted the circle of friends will probably be small, and interest in hobbies and other pleasurable activities lacking. The sufferer will be investing most of his mental energy in himself, to the exclusion of friends and other interests. The priest can help to take him out of himself, and turn him away from his unhealthy somatic preoccupation, discussing with him his conflicts and his difficulties.

As the priest talks with the anxiety-ridden he begins to see where many of his problems lie, and the point around which many of his difficulties centre, e.g. insecurity over work, relationships with a superior, or unrecognized and severe conscious restrictions which he has placed upon himself. This talking over his problems will give him much relief, and the priest can give positive support and encouragement towards leading a more full and rounded life. The individual's relationship to the priest will sometimes be coloured and distorted by the various difficulties and anxieties from which he suffers. He will constantly feel misunderstood and ultra-sensitive as a result of frequent rejections and defeats. Many will be extremely hesitant to relate and explain their problems. Others, again, will be excessively dependent. The priest

[1] *Pastoral Psychology*, May 1960, Vol. II, No. 104, p. 8.

must handle the latter with the utmost stability and maturity, and see that they do not sap too much of his time and energy. Much patience, time, and effort will be needed, and much will depend upon the relationship between the priest and his people. The priest must not be unduly perturbed by the setbacks which the patient may experience, for these will occur until new reactions have replaced the old. Every step forward the person takes will be helped by the praise and support of the priest.

It is not helpful, although it is unfortunately frequently done, to "lecture", pointing out again and again the unreality of their anxieties. A common element in neurotic illness is a conflict which is in the unconscious and which, therefore, cannot be dealt with through "reason". Freud said rightly that one cannot fight a foe whom one does not see. The neurotic personality is in the rather helpless situation of only being able to observe certain manifestations of his sickness, without being able to deal with the forces which constitute the unconscious conflict.

In dealing with these problems among his people, the priest must realize that the person is ill. He must remember, too, that severe anxiety is often more painful and intolerable than severe physical illness, and finally that the person is not consciously causing his own condition.

Many will feel they have completely lost their faith, and that God has cast them out. They wring their hands and feel convinced there is no hope for them at all, as they have done so much that was wrong. They feel they are positively the most sinful of all creatures, and many will believe they have committed what in their interpretation is "the unforgivable sin". So many are in despair of having to live at all. Their eyes are red, their complexion pale and wan, and their foreheads are wrinkled. Comfort is often fruitless. The most important point for the priest is the self-reproach of the sufferer. He has resurrected some false step in his past life, and considers he is no longer worthy to live. This false step may be imaginary, probably invented to prove how wicked he is. In this state of morbid guilt it is virtually fruitless for the priest to refer to the scriptures or any other authority.

Despite their shyness and reserve, these patients look for someone who knows how to find a key to their soul. They are often deeply religious and their brooding brings them great spiritual distress and despair. There is great scope for pastoral care in these instances, and if the priest can impart comfort, encouragement, and a sense of spiritual joy, he has done much to uplift a soul in the greatest affliction of all—utter despair and futility.

Much might be done by the priest's spiritual guidance in the periods between the bouts of depression and anxiety to encourage the sufferer to let himself go "and put his trust in another whom we have never seen, to seek an invisible hand, to believe in a heart that has passed through every one of our fears and now reigns above as Christ the Lord. God has promised that whoever serves Him will not be lost. To let oneself go and in the very midst of fear to trust another, of whom one knows only by faith, is to be redeemed from fear."[1]

OBSESSIVE–COMPULSIVE STATES

The priest will frequently meet this type of patient, for it is these states which so often invade the spiritual lives of his people. Every priest will meet some of the faithful who are never satisfied with their self-examination, or the result of their confession. They are never quite sure whether they have sinned or not, and they feel their repentance is never quite adequate. They are seldom convinced of the forgiveness of sins, and acts of penance become a source of fresh scruples. They have blasphemous thoughts and ideas during periods of prayer, or while they are receiving the blessed sacrament. Such imaginations are deeply resented by them, but they are unfortunately powerless to resist them. Obsessional neurosis has invaded the sphere of the spiritual.

The priest should point out in his spiritual guidance that these experiences of scrupulosity are the symptoms of mental

[1] Joseph Goldbrunner, *Holiness is Wholeness*, p. 28.

illness, and the less the sufferer fights and struggles against what he assumes to be his temptations the better. The less he concerns himself with his compulsions the freer he becomes. The priest should also remember that scrupulosity is a condition for medical treatment, for it is more often than not more of a psycho-neurotic condition than a religious attribute. It is not made up of real repentance, but is a "false mental worry".

Lurking behind so much of the perfectionist and obsessional traits there is often unconscious moral imperfection, and as Northridge suggests, "this fact gives a clue to the spiritual director who is trying to bring relief to the mind of the unhappy inquirer. His business is to find out, in as tactful a way as possible, what is the source and nature of the guilt factor that most likely is at the root of the person's problem".[1]

These instances call for the utmost tact, for they are among the most difficult with which the priest has to deal in his pastoral ministry. He should learn how to diagnose the danger signs in an early stage, for they are often first revealed in the confessional. "We know that these cases follow a special pattern; they present the appearance of being excessively religious. The priest has to be very careful not to be taken in by this; he must not co-operate with the patient in his neurotic behaviour, and, above all, he must not encourage his symptoms, thus acquiescing in his misuse of religion as a means of satisfying his disordered mind. The priest must never forget that, while the subject *seems* to be troubled with religious conflicts, his real trouble is a psychic disorder. . . . Accordingly the priest's first concern should be to place the sufferer under psychotherapeutic treatment."[2]

Such patients require a great deal of time, sacrifice, and patience on the part of the priest. It will frequently be found that the negative and damnatory aspects of the Christian

[1] W. L. Northridge, *Disorders of the Emotional and Spiritual Life*, p. 20.

[2] Erwin Ringel and Wenzel Van Lun, *The Priest and the Unconscious*, pp. 115 f.

religion impress these people more than the positive, comforting truths. Consequently in our pastoral care, one of our main tasks must be to implant in the mind of the sufferer an unshakable trust in God as a loving heavenly Father, one who comforts and strengthens his children. Often mere good advice from the priest will prove useless. In fact, it will sometimes produce the opposite effect to that desired. Without most careful and tactful handling the sufferer can be made to feel that no one understands and no one cares. Consequently what little hope he had is gone.

HYSTERIA

The hysterics are often the "*crux pastorum*"! They will cling to the priest and he must use the utmost caution, reserve, and prudence in his pastoral work with them. The disorder, as we have already observed, is most frequently found in persons who are not equal to the demands their environment makes upon them. They always want to be the centre of the picture, and have showered upon them all the love, sympathy, and attention possible. The sacrament of confession may sometimes have a valuable therapeutic influence, coupled as it must be with a true knowledge of self.

The sufferer should be brought to see that by this state he is attempting to escape from his responsibilities and his problems. There must be, therefore, a courageous facing up to the difficulties of life, and a leading on to a possible solution on positive lines. A good rule of life suggested by the priest can often help to restore peace of soul.

It must be remembered that in some instances these people are in real need of love and affection. "They are sick people whom we must try to understand, whose weakness we shall be able to forgive to the extent to which we understand them, and they are patients who deserve our sympathy and consideration; a sympathy and consideration, however, which must not come too much into the open, but which must protect us from being unfair to them."[1]

[1] W. Demal, *Pastoral Psychology in Practice*, Ruland quoted, p. 233.

In his pastoral care of the neuroses the spiritual adviser has a most difficult task. When the neurotic state spreads over the sphere of the spiritual life of the patient, ordinary, as well as extraordinary, means of pastoral care prove so inadequate. Indeed, if the basic principles of psychology are completely unknown to him he "stands before them without counsel or advice . . . sermons, spiritual exercises, books, experiences can only in rare cases bring about that wholesome shock which a psychologically experienced priest can take as a starting point for subsequent cure . . . they have one thing in common, they live their lives backwards, in inner contradiction . . . there is no straight road to cure for such people".[1]

Mental suffering is the worst suffering of all. May God grant to every priest in his dealing with such afflicted souls light to guide, and grace to heal.

[1] Demal, op. cit., p. 204.

5

The Priest and the Psychoses

Now the spirit of the Lord had departed from Saul, and an
evil spirit from the Lord troubled him.   1 Sam. 16. 14

And when he was come out of this ship, immediately there
met him out of the tombs a man with an unclean spirit,
who had his dwelling among the tombs; and no man could
bind him, no, not with chains. . . . And always, night and
day, he was in the mountains, and in the tombs, crying, and
cutting himself with stones. . . . And he [Jesus] asked him,
What is thy name? And he answered, saying, My name is
Legion: for we are many.   Mark 5. 2, 3, 5, 9

The more severe form of mental disorder, psychosis, can only
be defined by using many separate descriptions. It is an
abnormal mental state which cannot be explained with
reference to the immediate environment. If a parishioner is
depressed without evident cause, and remains so for some
considerable time; if he is elated without evident cause, or
sees, hears, believes things that seem to have no basis in
reality; if there is a change in, or an exaggeration of his personality, he is probably severely mentally ill. He will differ
from the neurotic in so far as he has less insight into his condition. He would therefore rarely go and consult a doctor,
and if he did it would often be for the wrong reasons. For
example, the police are talking to him over the radio; he is
receiving messages from cosmic rays. From the psychological
point of view, this mental disorder is a total retreat from
reality, for the psychotic lives in a world of fantasy.

CLASSIFICATION OF THE PSYCHOSES

The two main groups of psychosis are functional and organic. The latter group are all alike in their main features, since they are due to damage to the brain cells, either by poisons, germs, disease of the arteries, or to old age. It is with the former group that the priest will have most to do, and it is to these we shall direct most of our attention in this chapter.

The most common functional psychosis is *schizophrenia*, in which difficulties in adjustment have become more serious and far-reaching than is true of the neurotic states. The schizophrenic has retreated into a world of his own making, since to him the real world is no longer tenable. It is commonplace to find many deteriorated schizophrenics in the disturbed wards of our mental hospitals. It is difficult to be with anyone suffering from this psychotic state without sensing the peculiarity of his emotional relationships. He is apt to laugh when there is nothing humorous, or become irritable for no apparent reason. He loses all interest in friends, relatives, and loved ones, and shows extreme indifference to matters which formerly have been of the greatest concern to him. Situations which ordinarily would arouse him to fear, anger, or sorrow are now met with complete indifference. He can be told he has lost a fortune, or that his mother is dead, and would calmly remark that it is just too bad, and goes on with whatever activity he happens to be engaged in. Jung's description fits him admirably—"a dreamer in a world awake".

In schizophrenia there is a lack of harmony between the emotional and the intellectual reactions. This is apparent in a patient who tells one without any show of emotion that everyone, including members of his own family, is against him, or that members of the nursing staff of the hospital have perfected plans to torture him by sending electricity through his bed each night. Cartoons and articles in newspapers, as well as remarks on the radio and television, are interpreted as referring to him.

Auditory hallucinations are present quite often. The

patient hears voices directing his behaviour, or making re-marks about his life. Many of his violent acts are directly due to his decision to act on the commands of the voices that speak to him.

Relationships are difficult as he seems to retreat before every approach. He may have hallucinations, delusions, or even catatonia (see below, p. 94), but essentially there is an element of oddness, bizarreness, or strangeness. He is careless in his appearance, lacking in his sense of responsibility, obscene in his language at times, and increasingly suspicious of everyone.

There is a wide variation in the speech of schizophrenic patients, ranging from the mute patient who will not answer questions at all or respond to conversation, to the hyperactive agitated patient who produces a stream of unintelligible words.

It is practically impossible to fit any of the cases of schizo-phrenia definitely within a rigid classification, but the disease can be classified into three varieties.

Simple schizophrenia is ordinarily a chronic and insidious form of the disorder. There is a mental deterioration about the time of puberty, and this leads to a gradual withdrawal from people, and a slow deterioration of personal habits. There is gross emotional dullness, and deterioration often proceeds steadily over a period of years, until the patient finally reaches a vegetative state where he is inaccessible to any type of ordinary relationship with other individuals.

With early treatment, however, much can be done, as in the case of Mr R. Snaith, aged twenty years, who came to hospital as an informal patient having been seen at an out-patient's depart-ment by a consultant psychiatrist. He had apparently been en-gaged in odd behaviour, such as telephoning housewives and the fire station for no apparent reason. His parents stated that he had "always been rather difficult to understand". He was a well-spoken young man with a very pleasant personality. His school record was excellent, and his father who was a market gardener had hopes of him entering university. Apart, however, from the episodes of odd behaviour he began, rather insidiously, to show a lack of interest and motivation in everyday affairs. For example, he was quite content to be in bed in the mornings, just preoccupied with his own thoughts, "What do I want to get up for?" He appeared quite content and self-satisfied with a vague lack of initiative. He was fatuous and silly in his replies to questions. For instance, when asked how he intended to earn his living, he would answer with a chuckle: "I haven't really given much thought to it." He also adopted queer postures at times, but hallucinations were doubtful. He underwent a course of deep insulin therapy, and improved considerably with group therapy. He was occupied in the hospital factory and had complete freedom. He is now fully recovered and employed by a firm of seed merchants.

Delusions and hallucinations are more frequent in *hebephrenia*. The most distinguishing characteristic of this second variety is silliness of behaviour, and marked incoherence of thought, speech, and action. The behaviour is fantastic and bizarre, in keeping with the silliness of thought, and there is considerable gesturing and posturing. Clinicians believe that in this type we see a real regression, which is usually more malignant than in other types. The following case history illustrates some of the main characteristics of hebephrenia.

Miss T. Everest, aged twenty-three, was admitted in what might be called a perplexed state of mind. She was a single woman who had, being an only child, lived with her mother alone for the past ten years, her father having passed away. It would appear from the previous history that this patient had been "rather peculiar" since the onset of adolescence, but her mother had sheltered her to no mean degree. She had never had any boy friends nor in fact had she made any social contacts of any kind. Her mother was "flat" emotionally. On admission the patient was very withdrawn, vague in her replies to questions, and on one occasion pressed her face close to the wall for no apparent reason. She was quite obviously hallucinated both visually and auditorially. She refused food, and would not go to the bathroom because "people were looking in at the window". On one occasion she ran from the insulin department and had to be reassured and brought back. This was in response to hallucinations. She was inappropriate in her emotional (affective) reactions, often giggling in a silly sort of way. Her entire personality appeared to be incongruous and disintegrated.

Catatonic schizophrenia is more easily distinguishable than the other two types, and is sometimes separated into three phases which are marked by depression, stupor, and excitement. In depression there are delusions of a persecutory or self-accusatory type, and hallucinations are common. Symptoms such as insomnia, depressive limitation of activity, and withdrawal from environment are present. Any form of attention is resisted, and frequently there is refusal to eat.

In the stupor phase the face is immobile, and the patient pays little, if any, attention to things which are going on around him. Mutism may be present and often if a patient's arm is raised he will keep it there for a long period. Such patients frequently go for months without speaking a word, and refuse to make any movement so that it is often necessary to tube-feed them. Despite the fact that a patient will remain rigid, with no apparent interest in his environment, he frequently amazes those about him by breaking through the stupor to relate in minute detail things one never dreamed came within the sphere of his attention. Some patients are highly suggestible, obeying every order or command automatically, while others are so negativistic that they resist any conversation or order. Excitement is evident when the patient makes fantastic movements, swings his arms wildly, walks rapidly backwards and forwards, and shouts the same things over and over again. In this phase the patient can be highly dangerous, and may attack a member of the nursing staff or other patients in the ward. Often these two phases of excitement and stupor alternate.

A young man of twenty-three who had been employed in an engineering works was recently admitted to a mental hospital. He had apparently always been reticent and reserved, but had shown few definite peculiarities until about a year ago, when he began to behave in an odd and bizarre sort of way. He would go out without a coat in midwinter, and would walk along the street like a guardsman on parade, and would occasionally break into a trot for no apparent reason. On admission to hospital he was mute and rigid physically. He had developed this catatonic state some forty-eight hours earlier. It was almost impossible to examine him, as he was negativistic and quite inaccessible. In fact artificial feeding had to be administered. He emerged from this stuporose state in about a week, but was then very hallucinated and impulsive, and special observation had to be employed. Chemotherapy was employed, with very active group therapy in the afternoons, such as roller skating, dancing, swimming, etc. He is making a very slow but definite recovery, and now works in the hospital factory. He will need a considerable period of rehabilitation before discharge is contemplated.

The *paranoid schizophrenic*, or paraphrenic, is concerned that other persons are working against him. If he sees a group of people standing near, he becomes convinced at once that they are plotting against him, or about to poison his food or his tea. In work he is convinced that the manager likes every other employee apart from himself. He is inclined to be meticulous, precise, uncompromising, and aggressive.

It is often difficult to realize that these people are severely mentally ill until one particular subject, e.g. Roman Catholicism, Freemasonry, is brought up in conversation. It is not uncommon to find among them patients with superior intelligence and promising careers.

Mr Frazer, aged thirty-six, unmarried, holds a B.Sc. in engineering. There is no family history of mental illness. His father died when the patient was twelve years old. He describes his father as being "rather difficult". He was very fond of his mother, "She was a wonderful woman". A very introverted personality, he had accused the people with whom he worked of plotting against him, and the management of victimizing him. He showed distorted terms of reference, and began to threaten people because he said there were "underhand activities" going on. He was aggressive and violent at times, rather boastful, "They know I am one of the best engineers in this country and that is why they are jealous". In fact he is a highly intelligent man, and his work record is excellent. He appears suspicious and aloof and at times mildly hallucinated. He has very little insight into his condition, and thinks that it is quite ridiculous his being in hospital. He does not mix well with the other patients, and is very difficult to occupy. Everything appears to be below his dignity. Various methods of treatment have been tried, but with no lasting success so far.

Another common psychotic disorder is *manic-depressive psychosis*. It is characterized by conditions which appear to be the opposite of each other, namely elation (manic) and depression. Sometimes there may be only depression, and in others only elation, but the disorder can run through a course which involves the alternation between these extreme mental states.

Every one of us has varying moods of excitement and depression, but it is only when these swings of mood become exaggerated that they are viewed with alarm, and the patient is unable to carry on his life activities realistically. Although the number of manic-depressive patients admitted to mental hospitals is less than that of schizophrenic patients, it still remains a formidable figure.

The outstanding feature of the manic phase is excitement. The tempo of life is increased, and the patient moves rapidly, thinks rapidly, and gives the impression of being quite happy —often far too happy! It is in this state that the patient may repeatedly quote scripture, and talk about the Church, particularly if he has had a religious background. This gives rise to so-called "religious mania". This is merely a phase of the manic state of this type of patient, and is not a specific mental disorder as commonly imagined.

He becomes grandiose in his ideas and jumps rapidly from one thought to another. He may make great plans for travel, business, or investment, which are obviously unsubstantiated, writing out cheques for thousands of pounds, and planning purchases of large properties and great mansions. Sleep is often diminished because of hyperactivity. Although he may appear happy and humorous, he often becomes stubborn, irritable, with even violent temper outbursts. His delusions are ordinarily of a grandiose nature, and he may be seen as one who has let down the barriers of inhibition, and has given free rein to emotions that have for long been bottled up.

The reverse is seen in the depressive phase. Life becomes hateful, and an indefinable melancholy seems to tinge every thought. The usual cheerful and light-hearted person is transformed into a reserved, passive, and taciturn individual. His work, which was once interesting, now becomes a burden. There are, indeed, few forms of suffering so hard to bear as those imposed upon a human being in a state of acute mental depression.

The patient believes himself guilty of many wrongs and usually believes nothing can be done about the situation. He is usually dejected—he has disgraced himself, he believes. He is a complete failure and "a hopeless case"! He often speaks in a monotone, and questions must be put to him several times before he answers. When replies are forthcoming they are usually unintelligible mumbles. He is convinced he is the greatest of sinners, and has "committed the unforgivable sin".

With the acutely depressed patient, a common problem is suicide, for the long periods of torture and guilt suffered by these persons are apt to stimulate a suicidal attempt. Karl Menninger sees all depressed patients as potential suicides. The "will to live" becomes weakened and reversed, and the patient is convinced he is an outcast and unloved. Suicide can be a defiant act against society, or a hidden desire for revenge, and in dealing with a potential suicide, the priest must always seek the help of a psychiatrist, for it is far too heavy a responsibility for him to handle on his own. It is a common adage that the person who talks about suicide never does it. This is, however, not necessarily true. When a parishioner speaks of contemplating suicide, his word must be taken seriously.

In every year more than 5,000 people commit suicide in the British Isles. It has been estimated that attempted suicides are about six to seven times more frequent than successful ones.

It is a significant fact that the poorest countries have the lowest incidences of suicide, and that increasing material prosperity in Europe has been accompanied by a greater number of suicides.

There is considerable evidence that widows and widowers commit suicide more frequently than do members of an existing marital partnership. Single men and women kill themselves more frequently than married people, and divorced persons have the highest rate of all. It is recorded that more women attempt suicide than men, and more young people than old. This is quite contrary to what one would expect. On the other hand, more men than women achieve self-destruction. It has been found that the act itself occurs most frequently in the spring, in the beginning of the week (especially Mondays and Tuesdays), and in the early morning. The reasons which are given for suicide are, as Menninger shows in his *Man against Himself*, mere caricatures of the actual complex web of events and feelings which finally precipitate the act.

The Reverend Chad Varah, Rector of St Stephen's Church, Walbrook, London, E.C.4, founder of "The Samaritans", reports that the commonest problems of those who have consulted "The Samaritans" are lack of faith to live by, psychological disturbances, marital or other sexual maladjustments, and loneliness—"in the world's most populous city".

I. R. C. Batchelor and Margaret B. Napier[1] carried out a careful study of two hundred consecutive cases of suicide admitted to the general hospital. It was found that out of the two hundred cases studied, 58 per cent came from broken homes, 56 per cent were depressive states, and 25 per cent were psychopathic personalities. Many have suffered in childhood from a lack of affection, and insecurity, and were deprived of parental influence in their early formative years.

The priest in his dealing with the potential suicide must endeavour, if he can, to discuss the underlying problem of

[1] "Broken Homes and Attempted Suicide", *British Journal of Delinquency*, October 1953. See also Bibliography, p. 176.

frustration, which so often goes back to the early days of childhood. It has been truly said that there would be fewer suicides if there were more intelligent and sympathetic people willing to listen to the troubles of others. We must bring to these despairing souls a faith in the trustworthiness of God, and the worthwhileness of life—a faith that no power in heaven or earth can separate us from the love of God. Rooted and grounded in such a faith, we can then "be troubled on every side, yet not distressed; perplexed, but not in despair; persecuted, but not forsaken; cast down, but not destroyed".

To deal with the family of a suicide needs the utmost skill and understanding, for so often the members of the family will feel guilty for what has happened. There will frequently be strong forces of submerged hostility. The family can often be best helped by attempts to show that many suicides are the result of illness, and to get them to talk freely about it, rather than envelop them in gloom and silence. In this way they will become less depressed and guilty, and the full ventilation of their feelings of shame and guilt will help them to pass more naturally through their period of grief.

Involutional melancholia is a term indicating certain mental reactions, primarily depressive in type, characteristically appearing in the fourth or fifth decade of life, and associated fairly closely with the change of life. There is increasing worry about business affairs, or financial circumstances, resulting in extreme restlessness. Often the sufferer will be seen wringing his hands in extreme misery and despair, and weeping and moaning are constantly repeated.

The patient usually has a tense and drawn expression, and appears in the utmost despair with such expressions as, "Why did I do it?", "What is going to happen to me?", "I shall never be forgiven". Quite frequently he will refuse to take food, refuse to talk, and becomes destructive and violent. The content of his delusions will often centre on sin and death. There is much concern over "the unforgivable sin", self-accusation, and self-deprecation. The disorder is more frequently associated with the female sex, but is also fairly common among men. It tends to occur somewhat later in men than women, often in the late fifties, and suicidal attempts are particularly frequent, as in the case of Mr R. Brown.

> Mr R. Brown, a married man, in his late fifties, who was admitted to hospital following a suicidal attempt, was described as being a shy, over-conscientious type of man who, as far as one could establish, had had a rather poor relationship with his father during early childhood. His father died when the patient was twelve years of age. "I felt it was my duty to take care of my mother all my life." He is described as being very conscientious at his work. His expression was one of apprehension and fear. He was agitated with a good deal of psychomotor activity. He was restless and tense, and met people who entered the ward, saying, "My God! what have I done?" "I am afraid, doctor." He was depressed, anxious, tearful, and quite unable to concentrate, becoming a potential suicidal risk. There was no apparent foundation for his fears. He said on one occasion that he would like to confess to the police of the "wicked acts" that he had committed. Apparently he had stolen from a neighbouring allotment two cabbages some thirty years ago. There were some conflicts in his life. There were no children of the marriage, which was a great disappointment to the patient. His wife was rather a hard, unsympathetic person for whom the patient appeared to have quite a lot of repressed hostility. He did extremely well on electro-convulsive therapy, industrial therapy, and rehabilitation.

One of the organic psychotic disorders with which the priest will have to deal is *epilepsy*. Epilepsy is a symptom like a cough or fever which may be due to a variety of causes. The term covers a wide variety of attacks of which the commonest and best known is the major seizure or grand mal. In such attacks, the patient loses consciousness, usually falls to the ground, and shows a phase of stiffness of all the limbs followed by a generalized jerking. During this time he does not draw breath so that he goes blue and even black, may become incontinent, and bite his tongue. Following the attack he is sleepy for some minutes and confused when awake, but normally he is back to his normal self within an hour. In addition, there are numerous varieties of minor seizures, some of which are sometimes called petit mal. In not all of these might the patient lose consciousness and the attacks may last only a few seconds. Sometimes the patient has a warning or an aura, most commonly a peculiar feeling in the stomach, which he may sometimes experience without proceeding to a full attack.

As has already been said, epilepsy is a symptom in all cases and there are a large number of different causes. Contrary to popular belief, the hereditary influence in epilepsy is not very important except in relatively simple forms of epilepsy such as, for example, the so-called febrile convulsions or teething fits of small children. In most other cases, there is evidence of a scar on the brain and the part of the brain which is damaged will determine, to a large extent, what sort of seizures the patient will have. Epilepsy begins much more commonly in childhood than in adult life and the majority of epileptic children tend to grow out of their attacks. It is important to realize that in all cases of epilepsy there is clear evidence of a disturbance of brain function and epileptic attacks are never caused purely by emotional stresses or upsets.

In addition to the various forms of fit from which epileptics suffer, a few of these patients may also have other, more mental, symptoms. However, the vast majority of patients with epileptic attacks lead normal lives, have normal school records, and earn their own living. Those patients who do show mental changes with epilepsy are, however, a rather difficult group to help in every way. The various psychological symptoms associated with epilepsy include almost every other known form of mental disorder, but certain conditions are more common than others, particularly in those epileptics who have to be in a mental hospital by reason of their psychological difficulties. Such patients are often irritable and explosive, they tend to be sullen and paranoid, and unpredictable in their behaviour. They are often rather slow and sticky in their speech and may appear to ramble round and round the subject, making interviews interminable. Sometimes such patients have a period of frank psychotic behaviour that is indistinguishable from schizophrenia. Paradoxically, these severe mental changes often come on in adults when the attacks themselves are diminishing in frequency whether spontaneously or under the effects of drugs. But there are also certain episodic disturbances of behaviour that may be very violent and dangerous. So-called epileptic furors are mostly disturbances of consciousness following groups of attacks.

It should be stressed again that in all cases of epilepsy, above all those with mental symptoms, there is clear evidence of brain damage of some sort or another. This is true even in those patients in whom emotional factors seem obviously to increase the number of attacks, which is particularly often seen in children. Furthermore, the mental symptoms shown by epileptics are made much worse as the result of the attitude of society to them. Epilepsy is still a dread condition, and many people are ashamed to have epileptic relatives. Also, the popular belief is that all epileptics deteriorate, may become dangerous or immoral, and the drugs that they take further lead to their deterioration. None of these propositions is true, and epileptics, above all other patients, suffer from unjust social alienation. As a result, the many epileptics who have only occasional fits and are otherwise quite normal, often conceal their disability so that the few bad cases are made all the more conspicuous.

Epileptic sufferers are greatly helped by kindly understanding and an acceptance of their ways in an ordinary community, but there will always remain a hard core of difficult patients, who will probably have to be in some sort of hospital or institution. Many such patients seem to take a keen interest in religion, and are the most ardent members of a mental hospital chapel choir. In so many instances, however, the priest will find that their attitude is better described as "religiose" rather than "religious". It is found that a direct psychotherapeutic approach to such patients is rarely of much value, but a great deal can be done by advising those who look after them and especially by educating the parents of epileptic children in the correct way to handle their handicapped children.

For diagnostic purposes, there are now instruments which can record the tiny currents generated from the nerve cells of the brain. These are magnified and then recorded. The instrument is known as the electro-encephalogram (E.E.G.). A series of little metal clasps are fitted on the head of the patient, and the current from two of the clasps is recorded on a moving sheet of paper on the machine. A series of regular waves from the brain of a normal person come at a speed of about ten per second. Epileptic disturbances produce abnormal brain waves. In a grand mal there are very fast waves, and in a petit mal large waves occur about three per second. The main treatment is that of drugs. Phenobarbital is used often, particularly in conjunction with other drugs.

PASTORAL CARE

It cannot be too greatly stressed that in no circumstances must the priest attempt to *treat* the psychotic patient, for the latter *must* be under the care of a psychiatrist. The priest is not a trained doctor, but he can often make a very good "nurse" in supporting many a patient with his pastoral and sacramental ministry. He will soon find that considerable time and energy are often needed in dealing with the psychotic. He must offer friendliness, warmth, and understanding, helping the patient to re-establish contact with those about him. In his pastoral care the priest will often meet disappointments from negative reactions, and he will soon impair the relationship between himself and the patient if he makes evident any signs of discouragement or impatience. Throughout his ministry he should be cheerful but not cheery, friendly but not patronizing, pleasant but not boisterous, hopeful but not over-prophetic, sympathetic but not pitying, interested but not curious, encouraging and at all times understanding and helpful.

8

So often it is the personal and spiritual qualities of the priest that count for most in his contact with these afflicted souls. "I am sure", writes Oliver,[1] "that the extent of your power to help will depend, not on your knowledge of psychiatry, or even of dogmatic theology, but upon the assurance you bring to human souls that you yourself have been with Jesus."

The priest should realize that there are certain conditions of mental illness where his pastoral functions will increase the emotional tension of the sufferer, and it is of the utmost importance that he be aware of this. He must acknowledge that often he will have to put aside the minutiae of his classical theology until the medical and psychiatric treatments have done their work. Particularly is this so in the instances of depression which he will meet in the mental hospital.

In such situations, advises Bergsten, "the minister or spiritual counsellor must, for tactical reasons, refrain from any kind of religious teaching or exhortation. His duty, then, is so to behave that, as far as possible, the patient becomes aware of him as a reliable friend; one who care for a suffering human being because he is suffering, and renders whatever help it is possible to give to augment and support the work of the physician. . . . The person he desires to influence must be receptive and capable of response before his ministries can have effect. It is important, therefore, to wait patiently until the working of inward spiritual processes opens the doors of the patient's mind and heart to whatever message he needs to receive."[2]

In referring to the pastoral care of the manic-depressive and the paranoid schizophrenic, Vanderveldt and Odenwald are of the same mind. "Since manic-depressives in the periods of serious depression are not open to religious influences", they advise that "the priest should refrain from speaking of religious motives, from exhorting them to pray or go to Church or receive the sacraments. Only when they are re-

---

[1] J. R. Oliver, *Psychiatry and Mental Health*, p. 161.
[2] G. Bergsten, *Pastoral Psychology*, p. 184.

cuperating may religious means influence them for the better. In cases of serious delusions, the priest can do next to nothing. If the patients talk to him about their delusional systems, he should try not to go into the subject. This negative attitude will require a great deal of patience and tact. Religious paranoics especially may single out the priest as the recipient of their stories. They will tell him that they are the greatest sinners on earth, that they are damned for ever, etc. Any attempt to reason with them would not only be useless, but often harmful."[1]

Sometimes to the priest himself it may seem completely irrational to minister spiritual things to people who have no insight into their mental disorders. We must, however, go on reminding ourselves that however severe the psychosis may be, the sufferer is still a person, though often only in a fragmentary form. Our Lord came to heal the twisted mind as well as the diseased body, and probably more than anyone else the psychotic needs to feel the healing touch of him who makes all things new.

The best pastoral approach will always be the stressing of the positive elements of love, forgiveness, faith, and hope. For the priest, above all others, knows that it is by this means that the Holy Spirit will make contact with those deeply recessed realms of the mind which house the counterparts of these life-giving forces.

The priest must avoid the two extremes of over-optimism and extreme pessimism. On the one hand, he may feel sometimes that he is really getting somewhere with the psychotic patient, and will be tempted to look out for quick results. This may lead to extreme disappointment and frustration when expectations are not fulfilled. On the other hand, it is so easy to adopt the attitude of "What on earth can be done for these people?"—and pass by on the other side with an absolute failure to attain a fellow feeling and deep concern.

[2] By permission from *Psychiatry and Catholicism* by J. H. Vandervelt and R. P. Odenwald. Copyright, 1957, McGraw-Hill Book Co., Inc., p. 258.

The psychotic patient is highly sensitive to atmosphere and such feelings affect the deeper level of his mind very easily. He soon senses whether we care for him or not.

It is of tremendous help to the priest if he be allowed to study case histories confidentially, so that he may understand some of the feelings and utterances of the psychotic, and so enter a little into the "world" in which they spend their days.[1]

It is only by such understanding that the priest will develop the eyes and the ears to sense the real needs and unspoken longings behind much of the confusion and disorder. It is only by such an approach that he can "discover the sense hidden in the nonsense of the patient".

Much use can be made of the therapy of companionship. To sit with a psychotic patient, with perhaps no word spoken apart from a silent prayer, means more than we are apt to imagine. "I sat where they sat", writes Ezekiel in describing his experiences with the Jewish captives in Babylon. If we can sit where the mentally ill sit, we begin to share their experiences with understanding and sympathy, and their lives sink into our very soul. Even if the mind is unduly elated or severely depressed, the soul will soon know it is being loved.

The majority if not all the psychotic patients with whom the priest comes into contact will be in the mental hospital. It is therefore important that when visiting them he leaves his own troubles at the door, for these can so easily be carried to the patient. The priest when undertaking such visitations should be positive at all times, bringing only confidence and assurance in his bearing and manner. He must bring poise because he will have to be calm when so much around him is disturbed.

[1] If he has no co-operation from the doctor or psychiatrist his ministry to the psychotic patient will soon be stultified and he himself often frustrated. Much help can be obtained in this respect from the reading of such literature as *The Exploration of the Inner World* and *Out of the Depths* by Anton T. Boisen, *On the Receiving End*, article by "an ex-patient" Mental Health, Summer 1968, pp. 23 f., *Beyond all Reason*, Morag Coates, Constable.

It is always helpful first of all to feel the emotional pulse of the patient, and try to discover his emotional reaction to what is happening to him, for the important thing is how the patient feels about his situation, not what the priest thinks about it. It should be remembered that the patient is host, and the visitor the guest, and the latter should always behave accordingly. In ministering to the patient, he should remain emotionally neutral, yet avoid being coldly objective, meeting the patient on his own level with a warm spirit of responsiveness.

The patient's world is sacred, and it must be realized that there will be some who either cannot be helped or do not want to be helped, yet no action or speech of the patient must be condemned, no matter how abusive it may be. Religious debates or arguments must be avoided at all costs, for mental illness is an abnormal emotional state rather than an irrational one, and patients are not able to rationalize or reason. Equally unhelpful is the "silver lining in every cloud" approach—"everything will work out all right in the end", "you shouldn't be afraid", or "you'll be out in a few days!"

So often these are unrealistic and only tend to repress the patient's feelings and problems which need to be expressed, accepted, and understood. Unless the priest has a genuine love and concern for each individual soul, his knowledge of sick-visiting will be of little avail. "To the ability to read these human documents in the light of the best human understanding there is no royal road. It calls for that which is beyond anything that books or lectures or schools can impart and to which only a few can attain."[1]

THE PRIEST AND THE ALCOHOLIC

Alcoholism is one of the most serious of our social problems, and it is only in recent years that it has been widely recognized as an illness. The alcoholic is a sick man and he must be

---

[1] Anton T. Boisen, *The Exploration of the Inner World*, p. 248.

treated as such. The priest's approach therefore will be directed more towards the "sickness" rather than the "sin", and towards recovery rather than reproach.

The major psychological symptoms of the early stages of alcoholism is a growing dependence upon alcohol. There is no recovery for the patient until he has learnt that he must not have even one drink, for he can never become a moderate drinker. It follows, therefore, that the addict is never "cured". Because the addict's special reaction to alcohol appears only when he has already developed the habit of drinking, it is not possible to state confidently about any person before he commences to drink, that he could not control his drinking. Again, although certain personality and physical features are constantly found in people who become alcoholics, they are found in a varied mixture, all features being present in some cases, and in others only some of them.

Alcoholic addiction is four to five times commoner amongst men than women. This is due probably to the fact that social drinking is mainly a male pursuit. There are, however, other factors involved. More men than women have the required physique for this punishing illness, for when one considers the torture which these people give themselves, it becomes clear that only someone of robust physical health can stand the strain. The difference between a heavy drinker and an alcoholic is that the former can stop if need arises, but that the latter has had such a change induced in his central nervous system that his drinking becomes compulsive.

Alcoholic psychosis may take several forms, but the main types are *delirium tremens* and *chronic alcoholism*.

As the name implies, *delirium tremens* is characterized by generalized tremors, chiefly of the facial muscles, tongue, and fingers, and a state of delirium. The sufferer finds it very difficult to sleep, and if he succeeds, he usually has vivid nightmares. There are also vivid visual hallucinations, e.g. snakes, rats, elephants. There is great restlessness, and fear, and at the height of the delirium, frequent disorientation. Suicidal and homicidal attacks may be present.

The *chronic alcoholic* is an habitual drinker who suffers deterioration of intellect and character. There are characteristic physical degenerations and impotence from the poisoning of the nervous system is frequently present. No less disturbing is his moral deterioration.

The two main aspects of treatment are the need to rehabilitate the patient, and to deal with the social problem of addiction.

The specialized forms of physical treatment are antabuse, aversion, and apomorphine. The first is a drug which aroused great hopes and enthusiasm when first used. It is almost completely inert except when alcohol is consumed. When the patient has taken it for at least three days, the consumption of two to three ounces or more of whisky will cause a severe and unpleasant reaction. The severity of the reaction is proportionate to the amount of alcohol consumed. Apomorphine reduces the craving for alcohol, as well as causing a fairly prolonged aversion to it. Given by injection, it has a strong emetic action. In two or three minutes nausea and vomiting occur, and the patient feels prostrated for about ten minutes. Just before he is due to vomit he is given a glass of whisky. Apomorphine with alcohol is given every two hours for about three days. No solid food is given, and no fluid other than alcohol. It is a drastic treatment, and requires careful observation of the patient throughout. Other treatments include medical hypnosis, group therapy, and vitamin therapy.

There are several disadvantages to the use of drugs. They are not a real "cure" for alcoholism, and at best they must be utilized in conjunction with psychotherapeutic interviews. It must be said that both medical and psychiatric treatment have not been overwhelmingly successful. In gauging the results of treatment by modern methods, the *British Medical Journal*, 9 January 1960, reported that according to a World Health Organization Expert Committee the criterion of "successful arrest" of alcoholic addiction should be a minimum of two years' total abstinence. In a series of fifty patients treated at the Maudsley Hospital, London, only 18 per cent remained totally abstinent during a careful follow-up study of two years. Another 18 per cent, however, were abstinent for a greater part of this time, and 42 per cent maintained social efficiency despite light or heavy drinking. A recent report on the follow-up of ninety-four patients treated at Warlingham Park Hospital, Surrey, showed that one-third did not relapse, one-third relapsed (usually within six months), but could not be treated as improved, and treatment had no effect on one-third so that they had to be labelled therapeutic failures.

The prognosis of treated alcoholism tends to be more favourable in males than females, in older than in younger men, in the married than in the single, and in those whose original personalities were not psychopathic.

Any description of therapy would be incomplete without mention of Alcoholics Anonymous. Alcoholics Anonymous is defined as "a fellowship of men and women who share their experience, strength, and hope with each other that they may solve their common problem and help others to recover from alcoholism. The only requirement for membership is an honest desire to stop drinking. A.A. has no dues or fees. It is not allied with any sect, denomination, politics, organization, or institution; does not wish to engage in any controversy, neither endorses nor opposes any causes. Our primary purpose is to stay sober and help other alcoholics to achieve sobriety."

Although A.A. does not require any definite religious belief as a condition of membership, its programme of recovery is undeniably based on the acceptance of certain spiritual values. Its Twelve "Traditions" (so called) are suggested principles to ensure the survival and growth of A.A. and its members.

One of the basic approaches to the problem of staying sober is the "Twenty-four Hour Programme". It must be *to-day* with which the alcoholic is concerned—"to-morrow never comes". "During *this* twenty-four hours I must not drink."

There are two types of meetings held. The "Open Meeting" at which relatives and friends are invited and made welcome, and the "Closed Meeting" which is exclusively for alcoholics, where they can have opportunity for discussing personal problems and benefit from the experience of other members. These successful results of A.A. may be due to two main factors. It is an organization which gives the alcoholic a group in which he can feel no criticism is directed towards him. He is not made anxious or guilty and his state of tension is released. It also re-awakens a sense of his relationship to God, and modifies his self-centredness.

PASTORAL CARE AND COUNSELLING

The priest must first realize that "these are people who, because of their fears and inner conflicts, are cut off from satisfying, fulfilling fellowship with other human beings. Alcohol has always had something to offer these—the weary, the anxious, the lonely, the spiritual wanderers. It offers the illusion of unity with one's fellows, temporary deadening of anxiety, and the quieting of inner conflicts. Its relief is temporary and illusory, but available to many who have found no other."[1]

There are certain requirements which a person must meet to get well. He must want to get well, and have a capacity for recovery. He must be treated adequately, stay sober, and come to understand why he drinks. Finally, he must find a new life in which he has satisfaction as great or greater than drinking.

The average alcoholic cannot be expected to meet these requirements all on his own. He needs help—from the family, his friends, his parish priest, his doctor, and often from recovered alcoholics. He will often be found to be stubborn, unco-operative, defiant, and self-centred, and getting him to accept help is often a most difficult matter. Yet this is the only hope of recovery.

[1] Howard J. Clinebell, Jr., *Understanding and Counselling the Alcoholic*, p. 146.

The priest must understand that there is more to this problem than mere "moral weakness". It is not just a matter of will-power, for alcoholism is a disease. If the priest can instil hope, much can be done. At the same time, it takes great patience and grace not to say the wrong things. Until the person is ready to talk things over, argument and reasoning—and particularly censure—will prove useless. The sufferer will be particularly resentful of the "holier-than-thou" attitude. To him the priest is symbolic of goodness, and he looks upon himself as a "low, evil sort of fellow".

There are three things necessary for constructive understanding of the alcoholic and his problem:

(a) Alcoholism is a disease.

(b) The alcoholic is a sick person.

(c) He can be helped. He needs above all other an attentive listener, an opportunity to unburden himself, and religious assurance that there is hope for him.

In this illness the sufferer is both the patient and the doctor, for there is no real "cure", the only safe path for the alcoholic being total abstinence for life. This basic truth is very difficult for the alcoholic to accept, for it wounds his ego and is a blow to his pride.

The priest will soon find that "the whole process of counselling alcoholics is a slow tedious business in which one must be content with little success. The alcoholic lives behind a defensive wall of isolation, a wall which includes his grandiosity. Wearing down this wall is a long, slow process. The alcoholic will not come out from behind his protective shell until he is gradually convinced that there are substitute satisfactions in other ways of living. As the counsellor patiently holds the reality situation before him, he may gradually see the grimness of his alcoholic adjustment, and become ready to accept the help he must have."[1] The priest must therefore in his pastoral care refrain from a patronizing, condescending, or superior attitude, for fundamentally the

[1] Clinebell, op. cit., p. 199 f.

alcoholic is "not sick because he drinks but . . . he drinks because he is sick".

Infinite patience and understanding are essential features of the priest's equipment. So often the alcoholic hates alcohol, but finds he cannot live without it. The majority of them are tortured with guilt, and their mental suffering is abnormally acute. The most helpful attitudes will be objective sympathy and real understanding. Without this approach, the priest can indeed be the greatest obstacle in the way of help, for the alcoholic needs comfort, enlightenment, hope, and not condemnation. He needs the steadying hand of a rule of life, and the grace of the sacraments.

"No priest", writes Oliver, "with any experience will attempt to deny the value and help of the sacraments in such cases as these. The alcoholic who has made a fresh start, but who is suddenly overtaken by a period of intense temptation, can find a new source of strength and of resistance in his communions and his confessions. He has an infinitely greater chance of success in his struggle than the man who, without faith and without supernatural help, is fighting it out alone. When the unbelieving alcoholic falls, he tends to fall far, and despair is always close to him. For the Catholic-minded man, who after a fall, makes his way directly to the sacrament of Penance and then to his Communion, the fall is never so great, and recovery is easier, and there is no place for hopelessness, for discouragement, or despair."[1] If, however, the spiritual approach is mishandled it can play an aggravating role, and can so easily lead to a deepening of the alcoholic guilt. He will soon feel completely misunderstood, rejected by his family as a failure, and by the Church as a sinner.

If the priest can help him recognize the true nature of his problem—that he is a sick man in need of help, and that he should accept the responsibility he has to himself, his family, and his friends to find in prayer the inner strengthening for

[1] Oliver, op. cit., pp. 112 f.

which he had previously turned to the bottle—he has made a very important step towards the recovery of the patient.

To counsel effectively, the priest will have to become acquainted with the nature of the alcoholic. Why is he drinking so heavily? What are his emotional problems? He must not attempt to work on a basis of logic or reason, for the alcoholic is well aware how foolish and damaging his behaviour is. Excessive drinking is related to deep unconscious emotional conflicts, and in the background will often be found a high level of anxiety in inter-personal relationships, emotional immaturity, resentment towards authority, low self-esteem, and feelings of guilt and perfectionism. The essence of good and effective counselling is the establishment of a right relationship—a relationship of acceptance.

Fellowship plays a great part in the work of redemption, and herein lies one of the secrets of the success of Alcoholics Anonymous. The strength of the fellowship into which he comes, and to which he is welcomed, not as an inferior, but as an equal, is what is going to support him through his trouble. It provides substitute satisfaction to replace that of alcohol. Churches with a live sense of fellowship can give to the alcoholic a faith in the trustworthiness of God and a concept of providence which make him realize that he is not alone in the crises of life. Such a relationship is often difficult to establish. Often the addict will fear that the priest will censure him, pray "over him", and may also feel that the priest, not being an alcoholic, will never quite understand his problem. Many will come because they wish to unburden themselves, and the priest must be an attentive listener, for "talking it out" has a great cathartic value. The priest must not expect a quick and speedy recovery, for the road to sobriety is often long and arduous, and the traveller needs all the help possible.

It is with the families of the alcoholics that the priest can also do much valuable pastoral work. He can alleviate the shame, the loneliness, and the despair. The children of an alcoholic family are most tragically affected. The priest can become an understanding friend to all the members of the family, and try to bring them into the fellowship of the Church. As a result their social isolation will become minimized, and they will be kept within the confines of a religious fellowship. If the priest can point out to the family that their alcoholic member has a sickness which drives him to behave as he does, it will help them form a new perspective to their situation. This is of prime importance in securing the co-operation of the family.

One of the most essential factors in sobriety is to find the ability to love and to be loved. One study showed that at least 91 per cent of 109 male alcoholics analysed had a history of parental rejection or over-protection before the age of fifteen. The alcoholic is unable to love and to be loved. He cannot love his neighbour because he cannot love or accept himself. If the human heart is to be healed, love must be accepted and returned. The role of the Church[1] in relationship to this great problem of the alcoholic needs much earnest and prayerful study, "for the physical, psychological, environmental, social, and spiritual needs of the alcoholic must of necessity call for constructive teamwork between medicine, Alcoholics Anonymous, the Church, industry, and those willing to mobilize resources for the enlightenment of public opinion".[2]

DRUG DEPENDENCE

The World Health Organization defined the problem of drug dependence in the following terms: "Drug addiction is a state of periodic or chronic intoxication produced by a repeated consumption of a drug (natural or synthetic). Its characteristics include: (a) An overpowering desire or need

[1] The Carter Foundation, the Church's out-patient centre for the treatment of alcoholism, is at 34 Seymour Street, London, W.1. The National Council on Alcoholism is at 212A Shaftesbury Avenue, London, W.C.2.

[2] Dr Lincoln Williams, quoted in "The Christian Approach to the Alcoholic", J. B. Harrison, reprinted from *The Friend*, Vol. 117, No. 40, 2 October 1959, revised February 1963.

(compulsion) to continue taking the drug and to obtain it by any means. (*b*) A tendency to increase the dose. (*c*) A psychic and generally a physical dependence on the effects of the drug. (*d*) A detrimental effect on the individual and on society."

Although the problem is at present on a small scale compared with alcoholic addiction the increasing number of addicts and the "potential reservoir" of addictive illness is most disturbing. For example, the number of known addicts to heroin, cocaine, and morphine more than doubled during 1966. In 1960 there was only one single addict under 20; in 1967 there were 395.

As so many of the drugs mentioned below have recognized medical uses the term "addict" should be defined. The Brain Report (Second Report of the Interdepartmental Committee on Drug Addiction: H.M.S.O., 1965) described the addict as "a person who, as a result of repeated administration, has become dependent upon a drug . . . and has an overpowering desire for its continuance, but who does not require it for the relief of organic disease".

A distinction should also be drawn between the "junkie" and the "accidental" addict. For the former, his addiction has become "part and parcel" of his way of life and he has little or no intention of giving it up; the latter is often involved in fortuitous circumstances and can have a stronger tendency to abandon the habit.

Among the habit-forming drugs are the following:

Cocaine   When used by addicts it is either injected or taken as snuff. It is more commonly used with morphine rather than used on its own. Among its effects are hallucinations, euphoric states, and aggressive feelings, sometimes leading to mad frenzies. Withdrawal symptoms which are caused by delay or deprivation of the drug include periods of exhaustion, nervous irritation, and muscular weakness.

Heroin   One of the most powerful analgesic drugs known. It can be taken orally but it is usually injected in a vein or muscle tissue and puncture marks on the body will be much in evidence. Many addicts will take as much as 4–8 grains each day for weeks and sometimes for months on end. Apart from a sheer "slavery to a syringe" the risks of an embolism, overdose, malnutrition, septicaemia, loss of sexual potentialities are ever present. The withdrawal symptoms are most frightening and often include cramps, limb pains, and rapid twitching. Hallucinations and convulsions can also occur.

Amphetamines (Dexedrine, Benzedrine, Drynamil—"Purple Hearts") These are popularly known as "pep pills". As a group they are not addictive, but if taken in large doses they can lead to psychological dependence and aggression. They induce a sense of well-being, reduce anxieties and inhibitions, and stimulate an excessive amount of energy. Once the effects of the drug wear off there is often a feeling of persecution which can lead to paranoid overtones. Physical and psychological depression is one of the main withdrawal symptoms.

Barbiturates (Phenobarbitone, etc.) When these "sleeping pills" are taken in excess they cause increasing emotional instability and general confusion—symptoms which are closely allied to alcoholic states. Withdrawal symptoms include vomiting, convulsions, tremors, and sometimes hallucinations.

Marijuana (Cannabis, hashish, Indian hemp) Marijuana may be eaten, but it is more commonly smoked when mixed with cigarette or pipe tobacco. The smoker of "reefer" cigarettes becomes self-confident and irresponsible, with uncontrollable laughter and excessive talkative bouts. Later he falls into a deep sleep. Among the effects of the habitual smoker are the reddening of the conjunctivae of the eyes and the dilation of the pupils. There can also be distortion of both perception and sensation, and impairment of judgement. Sexual desire can be stimulated, but the drug can have an injurious effect on the sperm. Hallucinations can be caused by frequent dosages.

L.S.D. (Lysergic Acid Diethylamide) Commonly known as LSD 25, it is one of a group of hallucinogenic drugs which includes mescaline and psilocybin. These are not addictive, but they can induce changes ranging from temporary states of derealization to psychotic-like conditions. Their effects can be most frightening and disturbing and often characterized by loss of contact with reality and perceptual disturbances ("exploring inner space").

It must be stressed that the reactions to the habit-forming drugs will vary considerably with the degree of habituation and the constitution of the addict.

Addicts soon become indifferent to their surroundings, deteriorate in health, and become more and more dependent upon each other. The Department of Health has now set up official treatment centres (out-patient) at:

> Westminster Hospital
> St Clement's Hospital, Bow
> Charing Cross Hospital
> Lambeth Hospital
> University College Hospital
> Paddington Clinic
> St Giles Hospital, Camberwell
> Maudsley Hospital, Denmark Hill
> Cane Hill Hospital, Coulsdon
> Bexley Hospital

Emergency treatment only is available at:

> Oldchurch Hospital
> Harold Wood Hospital
> North Middlesex Hospital
> Whipps Cross Hospital

The Convent of Spelthorne St Mary at Thorpe, Surrey, specializes in the treatment of female addicts and has recently opened its doors to young drug addicts, a number of whom are in their teens. In the United States a voluntary organization known as Synanon has been set up to deal with the problem. It is a self-help association of addicts and its activities centre around a number of houses where addicts who wish to give up the habit can be accommodated. Like Alcoholics Anonymous, its members know what it is to "have been through" similar experiences, and they provide the necessary support in the conviction that only those can help who know exactly what the problem is all about. Other organizations at work in the field include Narcotics Anonymous, A.P.A. (Association for the Prevention of Addiction: Association for the Parents of Addicts), N.A.D.A. (National Association on Drug Addiction).

The priest should be familiar with the various aspects of the problem of drug dependence, the symptoms and slang terms used, so that he himself can not only support and communicate with the addict, but also be able to put him in touch with people and organizations who can offer experienced help.[1]

The first important step is to gain the confidence of and be acceptable to the teenager and help him to see that there are ways and means of living a full life without the artificial stimulus of drugs, so that he can talk freely and in confidence about some of the difficulties and problems that confront him. He must be seen as a person in need of help, accepted and not shunned as an "outcast" or a "misfit". Lasting cure of the confirmed addict is a most difficult quest, but the attitude of the community is all-important in helping his rehabilitation. Every chance must be given him, and a caring atmosphere provided where friendship and encouragement are at hand to support him during periods of crisis.

THE PRIEST AND THE PSYCHOPATHIC PERSONALITY

Here we are faced with the most enigmatic of all disorders. The psychopath or sociopath can be described as one who is

---

[1] Appendix B, page 20, *Drug Dependence in Britain* (CIO) lists a number of doctors, clergy, psychiatrists, social workers, etc., who are willing to help with teenage drug taking.

poorly equipped to meet the demands of his environment. His deficiency appears in matters of decency, and honesty, rather than in intellect. Indeed, he is often above average intelligence.

The definition arrived at in Section IV of the Mental Health Act, 1959, runs as follows: "A psychopathic disorder means a persistent disorder or disability of the mind whether or not including subnormality of intelligence, which results in abnormal aggressive or seriously irresponsible conduct on the part of the patient, and requires, or is susceptible to, medical treatment."

These personalities cannot be depended upon and seem totally unable to settle in any permanent situation. They seem to drift from one occupation to another, and often engage in general delinquencies. They are frequently guilty of criminal behaviour for which they may show genuine regret (a condition which does not seem to last). Sometimes there are marked feelings of inferiority with a great sense of guilt. They do not, however, seem to punish themselves but often force society to do so.

The diagnosis of a psychopathic state is far from clear cut, and exact causes are not known. They come into frequent contact with the law, and form an appreciable proportion of the criminal cases, and especially of persistent offenders.

Punishment does not seem to deter them and discipline does not reform them. Sooner or later their difficulties are overwhelming, so they unashamedly become parasites of the community, living on public funds, and absorbing the attention of the police, probation officers, social workers, and psychiatrists. In this way they find their way into mental hospitals, often seeking a place of refuge as informal patients, or because they have made an impulsive suicidal attempt which is usually, however, spurious and half-hearted.

PASTORAL CARE

Under wise pastoral care many can be helped by spiritual influences. "With the possible exception of the down-right cynics, the psychopaths are not inaccessible . . . if a sound and genuine religious life can be fostered in the psychopath—a task that will require a great deal of patience but it is not impossible . . . he will find in the religious ideals the motives for the reformation of his character . . . if we succeed in inducing the psychopath to pray and to receive the sacraments, despite his frequent lapses, there is solid reason for hope that God will do his share in the reform of the individual."[1]

The priest must be prepared to devote a great deal of time and patience to their spiritual care, and be prepared for many a disappointment. In many ways they are like babies. There is often no real capacity to feel anything towards their fellow human beings, and so many of them cannot keep within the bounds of social responsibilities. It was their lack of moral personality which led one psychiatrist, Pritchard, to describe this condition as "moral insanity".

It has been estimated that there are about 10,000 to 15,000 psychopaths in this country alone. Much experimental work is at present being carried out at Belmont Hospital, Surrey, where about a hundred psychopaths live as a community, with the main theme of treatment as one of guidance and not punishment.

THE PRIEST AND THE MENTALLY SUBNORMAL

It is important at the outset to distinguish between mental illness and mental subnormality. When one is mentally sick one's normal mental functioning is somewhat disturbed for the time being. In subnormality or severe subnormality a normal mental functioning has never existed.

It has been estimated that there are at least 200,000 mentally handicapped people in England and Wales. Mental subnormality is the largest single handicap of all. There is no cure, because it is not an illness or disease as such but "a life-long limitation of the capacity to learn and function

[1] Vanderveldt and Odenwald, op. cit., p. 312.

independently". The only treatment lies in the sphere of education and training, and of developing their potential however incapacitated.

There has been much research into the whole problem over the last two or three decades, and a number of hitherto unknown causes have been discovered. Amongst these are the influence of early diagnosis and selective diet on metabolic disorders such as phenylketonuria, and the discovery of an extra chromosome in mongolism. Research is continuing into the possible causes of mental subnormality and the steps that can be taken to prevent it.

In the Mental Health Act 1959 subnormality is defined as "a state of arrested or incomplete development of mind (not amounting to severe abnormality) which includes subnormality of intelligence and is of a nature or degree which requires or is susceptible to medical treatment or other special care or training of the patient". Severe subnormality is defined as "a state of arrested or incomplete development of mind which includes subnormality of intelligence and is of such a nature or degree that the patient is incapable of living an independent life or guarding himself against exploitation, or would be so incapable when of an age to do so" (Section IV).

Usually in the mentally subnormal there is an all-round inadequacy, with various grades of arrested intellectual and emotional development. They seem unable to plan for the future, and live entirely in the present. They appear to be less sensitive to physical and mental pain than the normal individual. Very common is behaviour of an impulsive kind, with frequent outbursts of bad temper. On the whole they lack initiative and the power to concentrate, and have very little sense of responsibility, and do not consider the consequences of their actions.

For legal and administrative purposes "mental defectives" (now an obsolete term) were formerly divided into three main groups—(a) idiots; (b) imbeciles; (c) feeble-minded—ranging from the lowest to the highest degree of intelligence. These terms however, were changed by the Mental Health Act, 1959, for "severe subnormality" covers, in general, those in the first two groups, and "subnormality" includes the higher grade.

The first group comprises those individuals whose mental ability does not reach three years, and they have an intelligence quotient[1] of less than 25 per cent. They are easily recognizable as they usually have physical deformities as well. There is little power of speech, and when speech does occur it consists mainly of unpleasant growls or grunts, or a few monosyllables. Many cannot walk, and those who can move about are clumsy and uncertain. They are unable to do anything for themselves, and it is almost impossible to teach them even the fundamental habits of cleanliness. They are unable to wash or dress and are almost "animal-like" in their eating habits. Their emotional life is particularly crude, and frequently they are destructive, showing outbursts of anger and fear.

The mental age of the second group ranges from three to seven years, with an intelligence quotient of 25 to 50 per cent. They are incapable of managing themselves or their affairs with ordinary prudence, and are incapable of being taught to do so. Physical deformities and abnormalities of various degrees are usually pronounced, and they appear clumsy and ungainly, although their motor control is much superior to those of the first group. They are able to protect themselves

[1] The *mental age* (M.A.) is established by testing large numbers of children of the same age and establishing an age norm. The average age of ten-year-old children is the ten year norm. These norms increase each year up to about fifteen years of age, and so a scale of mental ages is established. Mental age is, then, a measure of the person's level of intelligence at a given time. The *intelligence quotient* (I.Q.) is reached by dividing the mental age by the chronological age. Hence $\dfrac{\text{M.A.}}{\text{C.A.}} = \text{I.Q.}$

A child whose mental age is nine, and chronological age is twelve, has an intelligence quotient of $\frac{3}{4}$ or 0·75. The exactly average child of any age has therefore an I.Q. of 1·00, for his mental age is the norm for his own age. The decimal is dropped usually, so 1·00 becomes an I.Q. of 100.

from common physical dangers and can be taught to do simple tasks, particularly those of a manual type, e.g. bed-making, floor-polishing, etc. They can also develop some language ability, but their vocabulary remains very small, and they speak in simple sentences. They seem to enjoy looking at pictures, but reading in most cases is impossible.

The third group has a mental age of seven to twelve years, and an intelligence quotient of 50 to 70 per cent. In many instances these individuals present none of the physical abnormalities of the first or second groups, and are frequently thought of as just dull or slow without any recognition of the fact that they are fundamentally incapable of accomplishing the feats of normal minds. Under supervision they are able to manage their affairs, and get along fairly well if complicated situations do not arise. Their defect is most noticeable in originality, inventiveness, constructive imagination, and reasoning. In later life many become social problems, because of lack of control or faulty judgement.

There are a number of clinical types, whose defect is accompanied by marked physical abnormalities, which are so obvious that they can be recognized by the priest. Perhaps the most common is that known as *mongolism*. This is a name given to a group of people because of the close resemblance of their physical characteristics to the members of the Mongolian race. The skull is small, rounded, and the face and occipital region are both flattened. Their eyes are narrow and slit-like, sloping upward and outward. They are usually of a pleasant, happy disposition, and are easily amused.

PASTORAL CARE AND COUNSELLING

It is most difficult to have individual conversation with many of the severely subnormal, but much can be done in a group. They must be treated, as far as is possible, like normal individuals, and not merely as mental patients or inferior beings. The priest must remember that, however backward, the mentally handicapped is an individual who needs recognition as such. He must be protected from, and prepared for, situations where the demands made on him are likely to equal or exceed his capacity. Patience, tolerance, and reasonableness are probably the keystones of success in ministering to this class of patient.[1]

The first two groups are capable of very little spiritual response. Many seem to have a real appreciation of spiritual values, but are unable to express it in words. Most of the subnormal have strong feelings of insecurity, anxiety, rejection, and isolation, and greatly desire attention and affection. In pastoral care, praise, encouragement, affection, respect can be imparted, and marked positive changes are made possible. It is important that the priest should speak in terms, and at a level, they understand. He must, too, have a humane and sympathetic feeling for such patients, realizing the whole time that he is dealing with an intellectually limited individual. He therefore should be prepared to work with greater patience, in smaller steps, and with a greater number of contacts. Repetition should have great emphasis, and prayers and hymn-tunes can be taught in this way.

The priest can do much to help the families of mentally subnormal children, for the former often require more help than their offspring. Because of their deep emotional involvements (feelings of guilt, disappointment, underlying frustration) they need all the help they can get to achieve insight into some of their basic problems. Parental reactions seem to vary from rejecting the child at one extreme, to denying reality and refusing to believe that the child is really subnormal in his intellectual potentialities. This often involves the tendency to pamper the child, and give him all sorts of special privileges, thus inhibiting the development of his potentialities toward independence.[2]

[1] Much useful information about the care of the mentally subnormal is contained in *Number Unknown*, a report of the Children's Council of the Church of England Board of Education (CIO 1965).

[2] Parents will find invaluable help from the National Association for Mental Health, and from the National Society for Mentally Handicapped Children.

The priest has often to help the parent over the decision of either keeping the child at home or placing him in a hospital. No general rules can be laid down here, as each case must be judged on its own particular circumstances. Families must be helped to see that such hospitals are not places of detention, but centres of training.

Often the priest can be of great help where parents feel that they are being punished for sins, real or imagined. So often the priest will find that a parent feels that his own personal inadequacy as a man or a woman is the cause of the child's subnormality. Again, parents will often fear for their social status or prestige, and feel their emotional security is being threatened. The importance of encouraging the parent to express these feelings cannot be over-estimated. If they are repressed, the emotional acceptance of the child suffers accordingly.

6

The Priest and Psychiatric Treatment[1]

To cure sometimes, to relieve often, to comfort always.
EDWARD L. TRUDEAU

And they come to Jesus, and see him that was possessed
with the devil, and had the legion, sitting, and clothed,
and in his right mind.   Mark 5. 15

The present era of treatment of mental disorders stems from
four thousand years of human concern for the mentally
afflicted. From the very early days of the Ancients (Egyptians,
Jews, and Greeks) mental disorder was considered to be the
work of evil spirits or demons. In New Testament times,
exorcism was widely used for such cases, indicating that the
presence of a demon or evil spirit was tacitly granted, if not
openly admitted. Magic, charms, incantations were also supposed to effect cures.

Hippocrates, and later Galen, taught theories and practices
based on observation and natural causes. Unfortunately,
these ideas were not developed throughout the later years, and
for centuries the mentally ill were cruelly treated. They were
frequently chained, beaten, and tortured, for these were the
accepted punishments for the devil, who was thought to
possess the patient.

[1] It is beyond the scope of this chapter to differentiate between the
various schools of psychology, the multiple theories of psycho-analysis,
and intricate details of various psychiatric treatments. For a study of
these the reader is referred to any good textbook on psychology and
psychiatry. This chapter is merely intended to give the priest a workaday
understanding of some of the modern psychiatric treatments, so that he
may more effectively minister to the mentally ill.

The great period of a humanitarian approach to the mentally ill was characterized by Pinel in France, who struck off the chains of patients in the Bicetre (1792), Esquirol at the Saltpetrière (1820), William Tuke at The Retreat, York (1796), Gardner Hill at Lincoln (1835), and Connoly at Hanwell (1839). The use of mechanical restraint was greatly reduced, attendants were no longer "keepers" but nurses, and violence became exceptional. The recovery rate rose to more than two-thirds of all admissions. With Charcot in France in the mid and late nineteenth century there stemmed many of the pioneers of contemporary psychological treatments. Kraeplin laid many of the foundations for contemporary diagnostic procedures and organic research in psychiatry, and later came Freud, Adler, and Jung, and others who have led the field in their day.[1]

Today's battle for psychiatry is mainly directed against the superstitions of people who still think in terms of mental illness as something mysteriously evil.

NON-PHYSICAL TREATMENTS

PSYCHOTHERAPY[2]

Psychotherapy may be defined as "the art and science of treating mental and emotional disorders and diseases through changing ideas and emotion to bring about a more favourable psychic equilibrium". In order to understand functional mental illness it is necessary to find answers to the following questions: Why did the patient have a mental illness at this time? Why did it take the particular form exhibited? What accounts for the symptoms manifested? For the first there is usually a detailed history of the situation and environment during the

[1] For further information about the early treatment of the mentally ill, the reader is referred to the opening chapter of Dr Stafford Clark's book *Psychiatry Today*, and Zilboorg's *History of Medical Psychology*.

[2] For an excellent introduction to the working of analytical psychotherapy the reader is referred to Anthony Storr, *The Integrity of the Personality*.

advent of the illness. The particular form of illness is more generally explained in terms of constitutional predisposition and special habit patterns of the patient. The answer to the third question is far more difficult and is ultimately associated with the life experience of the patient. The methods of psychotherapy are varied and numerous. Some are rather specialized, others are used each day in quite an intuitive way by all who have to deal and minister to individuals.

In *persuasion* the psychotherapist presents to the patient the necessity for overcoming his symptoms, and convinces him by logical argument of the irrationality of his symptoms. In some of the very mild cases this approach may cure, in others it may help a patient to see the reason for his symptom, and this brings considerable comfort. Even if the patient cannot get rid of the symptom he can accommodate himself to it.

One of the oldest and most common of all psychotherapeutic approaches is *suggestion*. The psychotherapist implants an idea in the mind of the patient which is accepted by him without logical reason. (This differentiates suggestion from persuasion which is a rational affair.) The patient is put into a state of passivity and dependence with his criticism temporarily in abeyance. He is aware of what the doctor says, but is too lethargic to criticize. There are many methods of inducing this state, such as hypnosis, relaxation, and narco-analysis. The essence of suggestion is the prestige of the doctor or psychiatrist, for it is this which plays a major role in rendering the patient more dependent and submissive.

Sometimes *reassurance* is used to impart to the patient a less pessimistic and fearful attitude towards his problems and difficulties, and to help him feel that they are not really too serious. Like some of the other methods it does not get to the root of the original anxiety, but can be beneficial in calming the patient. As with suggestion the effectiveness of this approach depends much upon the opinion the patient holds of the integrity and ability of the doctor. Throughout the whole of the psychotherapeutic approach the psychiatrist relies chiefly on two features: the effect of a personal relationship between the patient and the therapist,[1] and the talking over of problems.

Many neurotic people, as a result of childhood years, form a faulty personality structure, and still retain many infantile characteristics, e.g. over-dependence on parents. With the psychotherapist they can work through their problems, find reasons for their existence, and have the opportunity to learn to express emotion in therapy. The task, then, of psychotherapy is to give the patient a setting in which a close new relationship can be formed with the therapist. In such an atmosphere the patient can use this relationship to explore his own impulses, his own values, and the pattern of his relationship with others. With the help of a non-critical expert, he is now able to sort out his emotions, feelings, and ideas.

Probably most important of all, he learns that there are things he can do about his difficulties with himself and other people. All this can be a most painful process psychologically, for probably the patient has spent the greater part of his life *not* looking at himself, evading his problems, running away, or indeed developing his various symptoms. He now has to search for new understandings and new modes of reacting and behaviour.

Not everyone is capable of exercising the required sympathy and empathy, even though he be trained in psychology and psychiatry. A psychiatrist may have all the diplomas in the world and still be unable to help people. Of the utmost importance are the personal characteristics of the psychiatrist. A sensitiveness in interpreting the moods and mannerisms of the patient is a great asset, for this intuitive knowledge is the most useful weapon in his armentarium. It has often been remarked that the therapist and his confidence in his approach

[1] Freud found that his successes in cures greatly fell when his personal relationships with his patients were disturbed. He considered that the personal, emotional relation between doctor and patient was more vital than the whole of the cathartic process. His doctrine of "transference" came from this discovery.

matter more than the therapy. The advantages of a spiritual context are manifest in the inter-personal relationship of psychotherapist and patient, for it is only with this background that most intimate and personal relationships find their true and full significance. In a Christian perspective the psychotherapist is able to understand the religious and ethical aspects of his patient's problems as the secularist never can.

In a purely humanistic approach, important and valuable as it is, man is left to depend upon his own resources. But if men are to become truly and wholly themselves again, they must be shown the way back into the oasis of God's mercy and grace, from whence they have strayed.

Although he may be familiar with some of the various theories of psychotherapy, it cannot be too greatly emphasized that it is highly dangerous for the priest to tackle such problems unless he has been adequately trained. In his eagerness to help souls in distress he must not venture into spheres which need expert and skilled help and attention, although sometimes certain facets do overlap.

The words of Paul Tillich, in defining the three levels of healing—the medical, the psychotherapeutic, and the religious—should be heeded by every priest engaged in such work. "The three (medical, psychotherapeutic, religious) are distinguished but not separated. Although in principle they are different in function, they overlap in the actuality of the healing process. This leads to many problems and produces many dangers. One must distinguish sharply the difference in functions for the unity in the person who exercises the function. The minister exercises the pastoral function, and he should never become a little doctor or a little psychotherapist. He would not heal in this case, but would prevent healing. Even if he knows enough to judge that a patient needs a physician or a psychotherapist, he should not and is not called upon to exercise the medical function himself. On the other hand, the doctor or the psychotherapist, although he may be a bearer of much spiritual power, should not impose religious symbols on his patient, either Christian or non-Christian ones. He must remain in the realm of medical healing, even if he indirectly exercises pastoral healing. The personal possibilities and the professional function should not be confused. Sessions with the minister may have effects on the bodily or mental state of one who is sick in one or in both respects, and sessions with a psychoanalyst or consultations with a doctor may have important spiritual effects on a man who is spiritually disturbed. This often can and does happen, and is even desirable. But it should not be intended in terms of professional intermingling. In this way, co-operation without competition or conflict is possible."[1]

PSYCHO-ANALYSIS

We have the first description of psycho-analysis at work in the famous collection of *Case Histories in Hysteria*, which Sigmund Freud wrote in collaboration with Joseph Breuer. It was found that submerged factors in the unconscious could only be brought to light by the process of much talk and of inquiry. During Freud's work with nervous disorders he wove his theory of psychoanalysis over a period of some fifty years, and his patients found more and more relief from this talking freely about their feelings, desires, and intimate thoughts. By the development of special techniques he found he was able to make the patient aware of many of the things which had been stored away in the unconscious mind.

His methods showed that the root of many of the troubles lay in early childhood, and probably the greatest influence of psychoanalysis, apart from the scientific developments in medical psychology and psychiatry, has been on the upbringing of children. Freud himself compared analysis to learning to play a game of chess, since certain concepts of power and movement have to be learned, and fairly stereotyped opening

[1] Paul Tillich, *The Theology of Pastoral Care*. Address given at the National Conference of Clinical Pastoral Education, Atlantic City, 9 November 1956.

moves have to be memorized, but increasing originality is required in the mid-game.

One of the main instruments of the psycho-analytical method is *free-association* in which the patient is instructed to say whatever comes into his mind, whether it is completely illogical and irrational, and even if it is embarrassing or distasteful. This reveals the seat of the disorder to the patient and the analyst alike.

The phenomenon of *transference* is also of importance in the technique of psycho-analysis. It comprises an automatic tendency of the patient to transfer to the analyst feelings which he has had in his infancy years toward important personalities in his environment, especially his parents. In a home where the father has been brutal and overpowering, the patient is apt to transfer hostile feelings which he originally had towards the father to the analyst and accuses the analyst of the same cruel and hostile treatment as he suffered at the hands of his father. Throughout, the analyst will remain friendly and understanding, so that eventually the patient can be helped to see the unreality in his feelings and behaviour. By gaining such self-knowledge the patient has the opportunity of controlling his symptoms.

An unconscious *resistance* is something apt to retard and prevent the patient's smooth achievement of maturity during treatment. Some obvious examples are forgetfulness of appointments, or not remembering what has been discussed in earlier interviews. The patient is usually quite unaware of the meaning of such things, and their true significance must be shown and explained to him.

Dreams, too, are often used to discover the content of the patient's unconscious, and are frequently interpreted by use of the elaborate dream symbols worked out by Freud and his followers. The images, motives, structure of the dream, all reveal the deeper levels of the inner self to the therapist. He often learns far more this way than from conscious statements of the patient. The patient's self-knowledge is also increased through understanding more and more of the deeper, darker aspects of his nature, for what the dream says is what the patient himself is saying. He is now introduced to new possibilities of dealing with his conflicts. This is often a most painful process, for he is presented with experience which for many years he has not dared to face, and a host of emotions, fears, and problems now emerge.

The dream itself may be wrapped in the most obscure imagery, and the therapist needs the highest degree of concentration, perception, and intuition in its interpretation. Archetypal and mythical symbols and images make their appearance which, as Jung has pointed out, can be compared to great centres of power, whose penetrating force gives the effect of great stars moving in ordered array above the stormy waters of contemporary life. A new vision of larger horizons is now opened to the patient, which communicates the comfort and support he needs.

In *narco-analysis*, by the use of drugs (usually a barbiturate-sodium amytal) a state of sleepiness and increased suggestibility is brought about. When the required degree of narcosis has been reached, the patient is either given suggestion, or else by lessening the repression forgotten experiences are brought to light, together with the discharge of emotion attached to them—a process known as *abreaction*.

The schools of psycho-analytical thought are varied and numerous, for there are many points at issue among analysts themselves. Freud himself stressed that "psycho-analysis has never claimed to give a perfect theory of the human psychic life, but has only demanded that its discoveries should be used for the completion and correction of knowledge we have gained elsewhere. . . . It may therefore be said that the psycho-analytic theory endeavours to explain two experiences which result in a striking and unexpected manner during the attempt to trace back the morbid symptoms of a neurotic to their source in their life-history, viz. the facts of transference and resistance. Every investigation which recognizes these two facts and makes them the starting points of its work may call itself psycho-analysis, even if it leads to other results than my own."[1]

The great help that psycho-analysis offers cannot be denied, but it is imperative that the parishioner should choose an analyst whose moral and religious points of view are sound. It can be spiritually dangerous when the psychiatrist is guided by a completely Freudian materialistic philosophy of human nature, for although the Freudian analyst is meant to be a passive bystander, "in practice he is often unable to, or does not, maintain a neutral attitude toward the moral values involved in the patient's behaviour, past, present, or future. Despite the theory of the thing, the obvious fact is that one cannot spend endless hours in discussing the most intimate problems of one's life and conduct with another human being who, whether he wants to or not, must stand as a guide and mentor, without being influenced by that other's fundamental beliefs about human behaviour and conduct. If his philosophy of human nature and human conduct is false, there is real danger to a greater or lesser degree that it will infect the patient."[2] The character of the analyst is also stressed by no less an authority than Menninger, who firmly states that: "We cannot ignore the fact that what the psycho-analyst believes, what he lives for, what he loves, what he considers to be good, and what he considers to be evil, become known to the patient and influence him enormously not as 'suggestion' but as 'inspiration'."[3]

GROUP THERAPY

Man is a social being and his primary need is for love and fellowship. There is increasing evidence that the major feature in much mental suffering is not anxiety or fear but the sense of estrangement.

In group therapy, the group is composed of approximately

---

[1] *The Basic Writings of Sigmund Freud* (Random House, N.Y.), p. 934.
[2] John C. Ford, s.j., "May Catholics be Psycho-analysed?", *Pastoral Psychology*, October 1954. p. 31.
[3] Karl Menninger, *Theory of Psycho-analytical Technique*, p. 91.

sixteen patients (hand-picked), who are encouraged to bring out their own individual problems in the group for discussion. Invariably, the more aggressive are most active in the initial stages, but as the group progresses, the anxious and shy are able with some encouragement to participate. The aim of the leader is to let the patients talk. He listens and attempts to understand what they are saying, while he talks as little as possible. He never argues a point, and never defends or counter-attacks. Ideally, any explanation should come from another patient rather than from the leader. Not only does this give to the patient concerned strength and satisfaction but it also leads to a better relationship in the group.

Non-verbal communication and cues, e.g. facial expressions, can also be observed, for silence is often the sign of fear, tension, and anxiety. The group members soon show a surprising insight into each other's difficulties, and learn how to cope with their own. Often plays are written, based on the life-stories of patients, enacted before the group and then followed by discussion. This is known as *psychodrama*.

OCCUPATIONAL AND INDUSTRIAL THERAPY

It was Galen who said that "employment is nature's best physician and is essential to human happiness". In its early stages *occupational therapy* was simply providing mentally ill patients with something to do to occupy themselves. Thanks to the pioneering work of Pinel in France (1745–1826), and Tuke at York (1732–1822), and the greater interest taken in psychiatry, occupational therapy is now part of psychiatric treatment, applied with the special object of relieving as far as possible the particular symptoms of each individual case.

Of recent years *Industrial Therapy Units* have been developed in the majority of psychiatric hospitals, where products are manufactured for outside firms on a realistic economic basis. Its aim is to rehabilitate the patient with the habits of normal everyday work in the community where it is hoped he will eventually be able to take his place in open industry or commerce. With proper factory conditions and facilities the work must meet the official commercial standards, and there is present the incentive for the patient to improve upon his performance. From many hospital units of this kind some of the patients participate in individual jobs in open industry or outside factories, returning to the hospital in the evening. This not only helps to restore the patient to the more normal conditions of employment but also helps to foster good relationships between the hospital and the community. The patient's field of interest is also enlarged and he is able to realize some of his potentialities. He feels of use, assumes responsibility, and his need for self-sufficiency is satisfied. Granted good home and community resources, discharge is but a small step.[1]

CHEMOTHERAPY

The two main groups of drugs are the *tranquilizers*, notably the phenothiazines such as chlorpromazine (largactic) and the *anti-depressives* which aim to relieve states of exhaustion, apathy, and loss of interest. Although medical opinion is still divided on the place of drugs in the treatment of psychiatric illness, these two groups have made possible revolutionary changes in the old mental hospital atmosphere, and because of them many formerly chronic patients have been able to return to the community. A downward trend in the number of patients in psychiatric hospitals is fortunately continuing. For effective treatment chemotherapy should be combined with psychotherapy, for as Guntrip reminds us, "valuable as drugs can be at critical periods ... we cannot possibly regard drugs as 'the magic cure'. They are a 'very present help in trouble' but people also need personal help for their personality as such".[2] Research continues with the hope of discovering an underlying biochemical mechanism of psychiatric disorder which might very probably be corrected with medication.

[1] See *Industrial Therapy in Psychiatric Hospitals*, a King's Fund Report, 1968.
[2] *Healing the Sick Mind*, H. Guntrip. Union Books, p. 113.

BEHAVIOUR THERAPY

This new theoretical approach to treatment is based on the behavioural explanation of neurosis. There seem varied methods of the actual technique for it is applied learning theory. There is the strengthening of incompatible responses advocated by Wolpe and known as "reciprocal inhibition". Another method is the aversive type of behaviour therapy. This is used when the symptoms evident in some form of behaviour provide a certain amount of gratification for the person concerned and yet are offensive to society as a whole —e.g., sexual perversion. The application of unpleasant stimulation sets up a conditioned aversion to the practice and its associated feelings, and the urge to avoid further discomfort is strengthened. Sometimes electric shock is applied as the painful and unpleasant stimulus rather than pharmacologically induced sickness.

THERAPEUTIC COMMUNITY

No longer are the more progressive psychiatric hospitals run on strictly formulated hierarchical structures for the traditional pyramidal system has given way to what has become known as the "therapeutic community", in which means of communication are freely established and the hospital run on group lines. The patient is seen as an essential member of the team and participates in group meetings with all strata of hospital staff. Open doors have led to better functioning and disturbed behaviour has lessened, for much of it was induced by boredom and frustration and by patients being kept behind locked doors. No longer are patients becoming institutionalized by being shut away or cut off from others, and the rigid segregation of male and female patients no longer exists.

THE HOSPITAL IN THE COMMUNITY

Out-patient facilities centred on the psychiatric or general hospital are now becoming more and more numerous, but there is a great need for the increase of after-care or halfway hostels. Day hospitals have become a feature of most psychiatric services, where patients attend daily to receive their treatment, and these are being complemented by night hospitals for those who cannot give up work to receive treatment, and who need supervision in a therapeutic community. With more and more community care being developed a great challenge faces each one of us. "If such after-care is to be provided on the necessary scale", writes Nesta Roberts (*Mental Health and Mental Illness*, p. 74f), "it is clear that it cannot be provided solely, or indeed even largely, by psychiatrists and psychiatric social workers. The kind of help needed by large numbers of discharged patients is not complicated therapy but the friendly interest and support of somebody with sufficient knowledge of mental illness to understand something of the difficulties in readjusting to life in the outside world".[1]

PHYSICAL TREATMENTS

ELECTRO-CONVULSIVE THERAPY

This treatment owes its origin to a Hungarian physician, von Meduna. In 1928 he began convulsive therapy with schizophrenic patients, using intra-muscular injections of camphor in oil to induce a seizure. His method proceeded from the questionable assertions that patients who have convulsions seldom develop schizophrenic symptoms, and also that the sufferer from schizophrenia who has convulsions tends to recover.

As time passed this treatment was found to be far more effective in dealing with depressive illnesses than with schizophrenia, for which it had originally been tried. Later there came an abandonment of convulsive drugs in favour of the production of an epileptic fit, by means of a carefully graded

[1] See Seebohm Report (July 1968) which states that "the widespread belief that we have 'community care' of the mentally disordered is for many parts of the country still a sad illusion and judging by published plans will remain so for years ahead".

electric current. This is passed across the frontal portion of the brain by means of electrodes placed on the temples. A current of 100 volts is used for $\frac{1}{10}$ to $\frac{2}{5}$ second, and shocks are administered two or three times a week. Further improvement in techniques followed with the administration of a short-acting anaesthetic and a relaxant drug. When the current is passed through the frontal lobes certain muscles twitch and there is a temporary alteration in the breathing. The patient soon recovers consciousness with little recollection of what has happened apart from the giving of the intravenous injection which commences the treatment.

The most spectacular change as to the duration of the illness and over-all prognosis has occurred with involutional melancholia, the potentially crippling depression that strikes a considerable number of women and men at the climacterium. Before convulsive therapy was introduced 10 to 30 per cent of the patients died through suicide or intercurrent diseases. The probability of recovery for such a patient was only about 50 per cent, while it is now over 80 per cent. One must beware, however, of the danger of substituting shock therapy for the medical practice of psychiatry, mainly because adequate psychotherapy is not available.

LEUCOTOMY

The term is derived from two Greek words meaning "cutting of white matter". In 1936 Dr Egaz Moniz, a Portuguese neurosurgeon and Nobel prizewinner, reported on the result of destructive operations on the frontal lobes of the brain. A series of experiments had been successfully tried on intelligent apes, whose frontal lobes had been removed or severed, and as a result they did not develop agitation in certain test situations, which produced severe disturbance in animals who had had no such operation.

Although there are different techniques by which the operation can be performed, the classic method is the sectioning of some of the projection fibres of the prefrontal lobe of the brain. It severs only the whole of the white matter, leaving the grey matter untouched. ,

Since the destruction of the central nervous system tissue is permanent, the choice of cases for this operation is a matter for careful consideration and selection. It has not found favour with all psychiatrists, partly because the mechanisms are not yet well understood, and again, it is an irreversible procedure.

The best results are with patients who, prior to their mental illness, were capable, effective, and well adjusted, and whose illness was of relatively short duration. It seems to bring much relief to those who suffer from obsessive-compulsive neurosis. If the operation is successful, they are relieved of disabling symptoms and return to a more normal state of life. They also lose some of their feelings of fear, nervous tension, and anxiety, and seem quite happy and contented individuals.

Although this operation has benefited many a patient in the past it is now being less and less frequently performed for more specific drug treatments are being discovered. It has been estimated that only a few hundred patients in any one year, carefully selected and reviewed undergo one of the more modified forms of the operation.

7

The Priest and the Ministry of Healing

No one has ever yet shown just what might be done to help these helpless people . . . by the use of Catholic Sacraments. Many of these partially clouded minds are capable, I am sure, of making good communions, good confessions, or saying simple prayers, and of coming close to God. Not even the greatest psychiatrist can tell what help those starved, dislocated, twisted minds might find in coming, for those few moments, into the immediate presence of Him, who once cast out devils, and who is still, although many physicians doubt it, the Great Physician of human souls.

J. R. OLIVER: *Psychiatry and Mental Health*, pp. 57 f.

Shew the light of thy countenance, and we shall be whole.
Ps. 80. 7

From an examination of the different methods of treatment used by the psychiatrist, we now turn to outline some of the forms of the healing ministry which can be used by the priest. Important as it is to have an understanding of the more common psychiatric treatments, the priest should always realize that he has aims and methods of his own. He, too, has his equipment and his "instruments", many of which are unique, to bring healing and peace of mind to those in mental torment and despair.

The religious and sacramental approach, however, necessary and vital as it is, must never be looked upon as just another branch of therapy. The priest is not just another therapist, for it is not his sphere to treat those who are sick. His ministry often does have therapeutic effects, but these are

quite secondary, although none the less important and necessary,[1] to his primary ministry as a priest. In leading his people
to develop and maintain their spiritual health, the priest is
also contributing much to their mental health. He is doing so,
however, not as a religious therapist, but as a priest. First and
foremost, he is leading them to God, and only secondarily
is he leading them to mental health. His sphere is spiritual
care, or the "cura animarum". Religion should never become
a form of psychiatry any more than psychiatry should become
a form of, or a substitute for, religion. As well as his own
"instruments", the priest also has his traditional language,
and this should not be put aside for psychiatric jargon or
medical terminology.

What is the part that the Church's ministry of healing can
play in this vast problem of mental illness? What can the
Church do to bring "the grace of our Lord Jesus Christ, the
love of God, and the fellowship of the Holy Spirit" into the
lives of those who are so afflicted and distressed? Psychiatry so
often finds that one of the deepest marks of all neurosis is the
lack of being loved for what we essentially are. The Church,
through its healing ministry, seeks to provide that remedial
love—"agape" (Christ-like love)—and heals with its gospel of
love. Some of the channels through which such love flows are
as follows.

---

[1] Cf. G. Bergsten, *Pastoral Psychology*, p. 188: "The crucial question
every spiritual counsellor must ask himself is whether it is more important that the patient recovers his sanity or that he be converted to
Christianity. If the patient's health is given first consideration, the counsellor may become too therapeutically minded, and constitute himself
an unofficial assistant to the physicians. On the other hand, the patient's
recovery should be a matter of great importance to the spiritual adviser
who cannot be indifferent to suffering of any kind, and who must be
aware of the pain and anxiety of the patient's friends and relatives.
Nevertheless, the counsellor owes it to his calling and to himself never
to neglect the question: 'What can I do to bring radical religious help
to this patient?' That is his primary responsibility."

WORSHIP

One of the more common symptoms of the psychoneuroses is the feeling that one is "apart" or "different" from other people. Often lurking deep beneath this symptom is a deep sense of sin and guilt. Through its worship the Church offers for estrangement, reconciliation; for fear, faith; for futility and meaninglessness, direction and purpose. In company with other members of the congregation the neurotic can be lead out of self-concern into a healthful and creative relationship with God and his fellowmen, for no one can live unto himself, and be healthy.

By means of the symbolism, ritual, and theology of worship the individual is helped to achieve integration and emotional stability in a way that no secular organization can offer. Evelyn Underhill once remarked that "many a congregation, when it assembles for worship in church, must look to the angels like a muddy, puddly shore at low tide; littered with every kind of rubbish and odds and ends—a distressing sort of spectacle. And then the tide of worship comes in, and it's all gone; the dead sea-urchins and jelly-fish, the paper and the empty-cans and the nameless bits of rubbish. The cleansing sea flows over the whole lot. So we are released from a narrow selfish outlook on the universe by a common act of worship."

In worshipping together, side by side with others, in thinking and feeling together with "all sorts and conditions of men", a satisfying and stimulating relationship is fostered. The aim of true worship is the losing of self and a deep desire to find God. Real worship begins when we despair of our own welfare, happiness, and comfort, and are lost in wonder, love, and praise.

SACRAMENTS

On account of their emotional significance, the symbolic forms under which the sacraments are received mean much to those who are mentally ill. Even to those who are beyond verbal communication, the symbolism can do much to convey a sense of the divine love and acceptance. In the sacramental approach of the ministry of healing, the priest has an opportunity of helping the mentally sick in a way no other can, but "the neurotic must not expect from the Sacraments a superior kind of psychiatry. For him they are the means of normality. They bind him into Christ. They meet all the major needs of his personality. In using them, he is using the means which will enable him to face up to life in the truest sense. The better he uses them, the more he approaches the norm, the closer he can bind his mental suffering to the agony of Christ in the Garden, the nearer he moves to the sanity of Christ. They work on him, not by removing aberrations but by emphasizing the normal."[1]

There is no antidote to anxiety, depression, and fear which can compare with the reception of the body and the blood of Christ in the *Sacrament of the Altar*. At the moment of the breaking of the Host, the mentally sick with "many a conflict, many a doubt" can offer up his broken mind in union with Christ's broken body, and pray for the peace of God which passes all understanding.

Even the partially starved and twisted mind of the psychotic does not prevent him from making his Communion, and the testimony of Bishop Austin Pardue can be borne out repeatedly by many a priest who ministers in a psychiatric hospital. "On a number of occasions I have held private services of the Holy Communion for a handful of patients in the wards, and always I have had a distinct feeling that God was accomplishing His purpose, for during the service one could tell that the soul was registering, even though the brain might not remember after the Service." Pardue goes on to relate how many people often asked him why he did this work and wondered whether it was not a waste of time. "My answer is that no more fruitful ministry have I ever experienced.... I

---

[1] Fr. Keenan, o.e.m., *Neuroses and the Sacraments*, p. 56.

repeat, that amongst the hundreds of those to whom I have given the Sacrament, and for whom I have offered prayer, I have almost never been without a real sense of their real spiritual benefit. Often it was more than a feeling or sensing on my part, it was a matter of knowing."[1]

The *Sacrament of Penance* is a most important instrument of the ministry of healing, and it is probably true to say that the priest can actually do more for the mentally sick by means of this sacrament than in any other single way. The relief of the confessional releases a great deal of tension and leads to new hope, peace, and assurance.

Sometimes a supposed mental affliction is simply the result of a guilty conscience, and what the patient needs is sacramental absolution more than psychiatric treatment, yet the confessor cannot take the place of the psychiatrist in cases which demand professional treatment.

In dealing with mentally ill people, we must remember that sin is not just a psychological fact which merely needs some psychological treatment, but it is a spiritual fact that needs the grace and forgiveness of God. Careful attention must be given to the difference between psychopathic guilt, i.e. guilt arising from psychological disturbance, and a real sense of guilt. Here the priest is careful not to trespass in the field of the psychiatrist. On the other hand, if the psychiatrist ignores the area of real guilt, he is overlooking an important element in human experience. The distinction is made clear by Hadfield in his *Psychology and Morals*. He outlines the differing characteristics of what he refers to as "moral disease" and "sin", and gives three tests:

1. Moral disease has a compulsive character, not characteristic of the sin which is deliberate.

2. Sin is under the control of the will, whereas the victim of moral disease finds his will absolutely impotent to resist it.

3. The sinner, as such, does not want to be cured, whereas

[1] Austin Pardue, *The After Life* (Mowbray), p. 50.

the victim of moral disease, if he realizes that cure is possible, is anxious to obtain it.

The "sinner" must be presented with a higher ideal and spiritually treated; the "morally diseased" must be psychologically treated.[1]

The primary value of confession is absolution and not merely "getting something off one's chest". Absolution by the priest makes up for the imperfection of the confession by the grace of God, and the priest can absolve the patient if he is as penitent as it is possible for him to be, though this may amount to very little.

Among those who suffer from depression there is often a desire for atonement of sin, and Keenan advises that they can be told very simply that Christ has done what they are trying to do, and that in confession he does in a moment for them what they spend their lives vainly trying to do. If they can be taught the use of this sacrament, this in time may be realized by them.[2]

Often the priest will find that the sacrament of penance on its own is not enough, but should be followed with counselling. It is so necessary, if our healing ministry is to be completed, to know not only what the individual sufferer has

---

[1] Miss Ikin in her *Background to Spiritual Healing* explains that the difference between sin and disease is a difference of responsibility. She points out that sin is a free, conscious choice of the will coinciding with a false or antisocial ideal, while in moral disease the character is determined by a compulsion alien to the real disposition of the character involved.

Victor White in *God and the Unconscious* (p. 166) refers his reader to the distinction made by the Scholastics. They term sin to be "malum culpae"—"the evil men do". It is a human act, to some extent voluntary. A neurosis is a "malum poenae"—"the evil men suffer, or undergo", something that happens to us involuntarily. "We may say", writes White, "that while the sacrament of penance deals with certain evil results of human *freedom*, psychotherapy deals with certain results of human *compulsion* with thoughts, feelings, emotions, conflicts, patterns of behaviour which the patient 'cannot help', which are uncontrollable by his will and usually clean contrary to it."

[2] Keenan, op. cit.

done, but *why* he has done it. During the act of the sacrament it is difficult to deal with the underlying motives and problems of the disturbed mind. With a firm psychological knowledge much can be done for the penitent during a "follow-up" period.

There are naturally points of similarity between the sacrament of penance and psychotherapy, for the need of catharsis in so many cases of mental illness is indeed imperative. It is Jung who tells us that "there appears to exist something which may be called the conscience of the human race, which metes out its own punishment to everyone who does not somewhere, at some time, restrain his pride in his own virtue and abstain from self-justification by making a confession of his own short-comings". It is when psychotherapy is looked upon as a substitute for a sacramental confession that the priest must take a firm stand. When once it is asserted that sin is a myth and religion an illusion, human responsibility and guilt are denied. The following differences might be noted.

1. Our Lord himself instituted the sacrament of penance—"Whose sins ye remit . . .". Psychotherapy is man-made. There is great moral courage needed before we can go down on our knees and say with utter sincerity, "Father, I have sinned . . .".

2. The sacrament of penance is under seal, and absolutely secret. This is of great help to a penitent soul, who has then no fear of a past or present situation becoming a "case history".

3. Confession is made to a priest—a representative of the moral order which the penitent has violated. The priest has been commissioned by our Lord and stands *in loco Dei* to grant absolution to the penitent whose sins affect all the members of Christ's mystical body. The psychotherapist or analyst, on the other hand, is the recipient of the patient's ambivalent feelings (the process known as "transference").

4. In the sacrament of penance there is an ideal for which to strive, for confession consists of contrition, confession, and *amendment*. It is not just a return to "normality", to a "statis-

tical average" or a conforming with "the standards of the community", and with a fresh sense of confidence for everyday living. The priest in his capacity of confessor can impart a sense of being loved and valued, with a serenity not based on a conception of "ordinary man", but on the personality of Christ himself. There is all the difference in the world between having our sins forgiven, and having them explained away! It was Rudolf Allers who compared the consulting-room to a research centre, and the confessional to a tribunal. The one can never take the place of the other.

The *Sacrament of Holy Unction*, a recognized apostolic practice, giving grace to withstand the assault of the evil one, and inner liberation from the power of sin and disharmony of soul, can mean much to the mentally ill. The definite feel of the holy oil, as the sign of the Cross is made on the forehead inspires courage and confidence. It should never be administered without very careful instruction and preparation, which should include an act of penitence.

Unless there is some attempt to get at the real causes of mental distress, the use of this sacrament with neurotic personalities can be most unhealthy. Miss Ikin outlines some of these dangers when she writes in her *New Concepts of Healing* that, "cure by Unction . . . in these cases (i.e. diseases of psychogenic origin) while it may, and frequently does, give startling and dramatic results, may leave the sufferer spiritually in an even worse case, believing himself or herself so spiritually blessed by God that the egoism, so frequently at the base of this type of disorder, is strengthened instead of cured. The point cannot be overstressed at present. The danger of loss of mental balance following the application of so-called spiritual healing is very real. There must be intelligent insight into the mental, moral, and spiritual state of the patient, if spiritual healing is to be effective in the sense of restoring true health of spirit in right relation to the Divine in which our human spirits are rooted."[1]

[1] Op. cit., p. 59.

The sacramental act of the *Laying on of Hands* is open to the same dangers, but yet can be administered with great effectiveness, either according to the official form of service issued by Convocation, or in an informal way. A deep sense of peace and calm usually follows, and those who are mentally ill can find much help from the priest's administration. To avoid all danger of misinterpretation and "person-centredness" it is often good to make it a corporate act whenever practicable, with a few of the faithful present upholding in prayer both priest and patient.

Each mentally sick person must be considered separately regarding the ministration of the sacraments.[1] Often the best approach of the priest is the psychological method. By suggestion he can lead up to direct ministration. Often among the psychotic patients direct ministration is practically impossible, but silent prayer can be offered up, and eventually by suggestion they can sometimes proceed to the laying on of hands.

Both neurotic and psychotic patients are deeply sensitive, and our *prayers and meditations* will have effect upon the deeper level of their minds. It is important, therefore, that they be free from all negative and depressing thoughts. Affirmations from scripture or short arrow prayers, can be used with great benefit and often far more can be achieved through meditation and intercessory prayer in the parish church or hospital chapel than through personal contact or visiting. So often the answer to the problem of mental suffering lies in that peace in oneself which comes from God. There is no peace except that which passes understanding. It is for us to be priests in whom others can see God's peace present, for this will alleviate them of much of their isolation, loneliness, and despair.

Short passages from the *Bible* can be read, which the

[1] Often the patient will feel convinced that he is far too "guilty" or "evil" to partake of Holy Communion. If he is coerced into receiving frequently, more harm than good is done, for he will feel he has received the sacrament "unworthily", and his sense of guilt is further increased.

patient can repeat to himself and turn over in his mind throughout the day or during the long hours of a sleepless night. The priest must be selective to a strict degree and must know when they will be helpful, stressing the passages of scripture which give hope and peace and joy to the tormented and restless mind. A few examples might be listed.[1]

Courage
Though I am sometimes afraid, yet put I my trust in thee. Ps. 56. 3.

Confidence in God
The Lord is my Shepherd . . . I will fear no evil. Ps. 23.
He that dwelleth in the secret place of the most High shall abide under the shadow of the Almighty. . . . Ps. 91.

Release from Anxiety
Come unto me all ye that are weary and I will give you rest. Matt. 11. 28.

Peace of Mind
You can rest the weight of all your anxieties upon him, for you are always in his care. 1 Pet. 5. 7 (J. B. Phillip's translation).

The great value of selected Bible reading for mentally ill people is well borne out in the words of one psychiatrist who said that "of all phases of the reading cure which have been attended with surprising results, I must first mention the therapeutic study of the Bible. Many nervous patients who are spiritually starved, mentally underfed, find great help and encouragement in daily systematic reading. Many are victims of fear and worry because they fail properly to maintain their spiritual nutrition. As our prescriptions, memories, emotions, and thoughts control our bodies, so our unthought aspirations, our unsatisfied spiritual yearnings—these indefinable spiritual experiences within us, which taken altogether, we commonly call the soul—in turn contribute

[1] Useful lists can be found in the 1928 Prayer Book, "Office of Visitation of the Sick", and in *The Priest's Vade Mecum*.

balance, direction, and inspiration to our intellectual life. The majority of people liberally feed their bodies, and many make generous provision for their mental nourishment, but the vast majority leave the soul to starve, paying little attention to their spiritual nutrition. As a result, the spiritual nature is so weakened that it is unable to exercise that restraining influence over the mind which would enable it to surmount its difficulties and maintain an atmosphere above conflict and despondency."

Through his *preaching* the priest has a wonderful opportunity to bring Almighty God into the hearts of those who are despondent and distressed. This can only be done, however, by means of a language which is full of meaning and significance for the circumstances and environment in which at present they find themselves. He will shun at all costs phrases couched in psychological terminology, for in the psychiatric hospital chapel he does not preach as a religious therapist, neither does he speak down to his congregation in over-simplified language. Nor is it necessary for the priest to dwell continually on the themes of sickness and suffering. The seasons of the Church's year and their message are observed in the same way as in the local parish church.

It is the first duty of the priest to preach the Word of God, for he is a priest, a representative of God, speaking to his people. In the setting of the psychiatric hospital over-emphasis on such topics as hell and punishment can be most disturbing, not to say in many instances definitely harmful. Rather let attention be given to the doctrine of love and the positive values of religion, which offer freedom from frustration and give confidence to those who are at present experiencing the effects of the strain and stress of modern-day living. If the sermon demonstrates faith, understanding, power, health, it becomes energizing and vital.

When preaching to the mentally disturbed, the priest must have complete confidence in himself, and both his voice and intonation are most important. They should inspire confidence and inspiration as well as imply interest and concern for those who listen. If this is the case, the sermon can often play a vital role in helping the distressed back to a useful and happy life.

Many of the congregation will feel lonely and abandoned, prone to despair. Such continual broodings make it difficult for them to visualize God as a heavenly Father of love and forgiveness. They will be able to find much help and comfort from hearing about the immanence of God, his divine companionship and the communion of saints, etc. In low self-esteem, the realization of being created by God and precious in his sight, regardless of how intelligent and clever one might be, brings constant assurance of one's worth, and confidence that God will not cast us aside, "but will use each one of us as a piece of priceless mosaic in the design of His universe".[1]

The question is often asked: if religion plays such an important part in the whole field of mental health, why are there so many people who are devout and religious, and yet neither well-adjusted nor mentally healthy? Let it be stated at the outset that sanctity is no guarantee of mental stability. In many instances in the lives of the saints we find emotional turmoil and sometimes even a lack of peace of mind. Again, there are many non-religious people who to all intents and purposes are well-adjusted and secure.

Religion can only be salutary to mental health when it offers enduring values that foster personal growth and integration. There can be no over-simplified, free and easy solutions to mental health problems. Piety is not all-sufficient or a panacea against a psychic disorder, neither will religion eliminate the need for psychiatry. The normal treatment for mental illness must always be that outlined in the previous chapter. To think that prayer and sacrament, necessary and holy as they are, will put everything in order, no matter how desolate and depressed the state of mind, is to create an antithesis between nature and grace, and the priest is wise to

[1] J.L.Liebman, *Peace of Mind*, p. 104

bear in mind that "there are cases where the very words 'God' or 'religion' have to be left out, since the patient's contact with them has been of such a perversion of religion and has implied such a caricature of God, that the renewal of the contact with God has to come in very simple everyday channels, without, at any rate for a long time, any direct realization that they are in touch with God at all".[1]

Again, an irrational, emotional type of religion, far from being preventive, can so easily become conducive to the creation of mental disorders. There can be dangerous neurotic tendencies in a religion which separates one from, rather than strengthen one's attachment to, one's fellow-men. The garments of religion can often conceal a false religiosity.

In a study made of the *Hindering and Helping Powers of Religion* among mentally ill people, Wayne Oates reports that many "tended to use religion as a means of allaying anxiety and comforting themselves ... they tended to depend upon prayer to help them get to sleep ... to ward off nameless dreads and to calm their nerves in many ways". "Religion", he suggests, "was less of an ethical concern and more of a means of reassurance, less of a demanding power and more of an attempt at releasing tension."[2] Oates quotes Karl Menninger who comments that "from the standpoint of the psychiatrist a religion which merely ministers to the unconscious repudiation of reality ... cannot be regarded as anything other than a neurotic or psychotic system".[3]

There can only be a fundamental relation between religion and mental health "when God holds the position of supreme importance in a person's life", for then "that man has a purpose to live for and therefore understands the meaning of life and his own destiny. Such knowledge is of immense value for mental health ... [and it] gives the truly religious man a

---

[1] Graham Ikin, *New Concepts of Healing*, p. 54.
[2] Wayne Oates, *Religious Factors in Mental Illness*, Ch. I.
[3] Oates, op. cit., p. 31.

sense of submissiveness and resignation as well as satisfaction with his lot, peace of soul and happiness."[1]

Of prime importance in the whole sphere of the ministry of healing is the spiritual life of the priest. If he ministers as a whole-time chaplain to a psychiatric hospital he is faced with a great challenge, although in the main his work is the same as that of the priest in the parish. In hospital both his personality traits and his whole priestly character are much in prominence, for he works in a blaze of publicity, with every patient watching. He must, therefore, be conscious of a deep sense of vocation and mission, for the value of his example is immeasurable. His patients should see him as a recognizable minister of God, testifying at all times to the fact of God's overruling power and love.

He will respect the members of the medical staff with whom he works, and give full co-operation to all the efforts made by the various departments towards the rehabilitation of the patient, while at the same time cherishing his own sacramental ministry as a priest of God. The more he tries to imitate these other disciplines, the less of a priest he will become. Working together, respecting each other's functions, and willing to learn from each other, each can then fulfil his own functions and contribute most effectively to those under his care.

Equally important is the emotional life of the priest, for if he is not emotionally stable himself he will accomplish little in an environment which is abnormal. He must be prepared to give much of himself and often at a greater cost than he might sometimes wish. One patient put it poignantly when she exclaimed, "I think I like you but I don't know—you're all hidden away where I can't reach you. . . . Why do you keep what we need the most from us—yourself? Don't you know that if you don't give us something of yourself as a person you

[1] By permission from *Psychiatry and Catholicism* by J. H. Vanderveldt and R. P. Odenwald. Copyright. McGraw-Hill Book Co., Inc., p. 183.

can't mean anything to us as a chaplain?"[1] It goes without saying that he "must have good nerves, great patience, and a strong consistent will, in addition to strong suggestibility, since he must contribute to the cure of the patient's defective will by the application of his own healthy will". His constant prayer must be "for self-sanctification, and for grace to strive after perfect love and charity, a love that wishes to be 'all things to all men', a love that bears everything in a spirit of unselfishness, a love that believes all, hopes all, suffers all, and never falters".[2]

[1] *Ministering to Deeply Troubled People*, Ernest E. Bruder. Prentice-Hall Inc., Englewood Cliffs, N.J., p. 63.
[2] W. Demal, *Pastoral Psychology in Practice*, p. 238.

8

The Priest and the Psychiatrist

As man is body, mind, and spirit, and health depends
upon the harmonious functioning of the whole man, the
tasks of medicine and the Church are inseparable; co-
operation thus comes into line with Christ's charge to
his disciples to heal and preach.

Divine Healing and Co-operation Between
Doctors and Clergy, B.M.A., p. 46

Give place to the physician, for the Lord hath created
him; let him not go from thee, for thou hast need of him.

Ecclus. 38. 12

Statistics of mental illness and emotional disorders are
staggering, and facts and figures are apt to roll rather easily
off the tongue without our realizing the heartaches, the
broken homes, and the blighted lives of children involved,
quite apart from the torments of mind experienced by the
sufferers themselves. The problem seems to be growing far
too vast for the psychiatrist, the social worker, or the priest
alone.

The Greek lexicon suggests three meanings for the root
word "psyche":

(*a*) breath, especially the sign of life; life; spirit;
(*b*) the soul of man, as opposed to the body;
(*c*) the soul, mind, reasoning, understanding.

To the careful observer here is an implicit suggestion, that
psychiatry has to deal with the religious and spiritual as well
as the mental and pathological. Unfortunately, however,
there is still a general reluctance on the part of many to come

to grips with the fundamental concepts which affect both spheres.

There are those who state quite happily that there can be no problem about co-operation as many priests and psychiatrists now meet together in a most friendly manner and have periodical discussions. The psychiatrist is a "good fellow", comes to church when he can, and sometimes even refers a few patients to their parish priest. The priest is quite "human", and often consults the psychiatrist. Platitudes are expressed as to the good work the other does, and all appears well. All we need know apparently is where to draw the line between the domain of the psychiatrist and that of the priest.

"Clergymen of all faiths", stated Karl Stern, the eminent Roman Catholic psychiatrist, "have dealt with psychiatry in sermons and lectures, books and pamphlets. Too often, they say something like this: If there were only more faith in the world, people would not be nearly as neurotic as they are. This is an over-simplification. I can show you a number of happy atheists who have never known a sleepless night; and many, good, even saintly, people, who are haunted by terrible states of anxiety and melancholia. That formula not only does not work, but is also morally wrong. From many of the books and talks of clergymen on psychiatry the lay person gets the impression that the psychiatric patient must choose between the psychiatrist's office and the confessional, or the psychiatric textbook and the Gospel. It is erroneous to give such impressions", continued the writer, for "by this attitude religion becomes a sort of mental bandage which must not be missing in any well-equipped psychiatric first-aid kit. I mean only to say that the clear distinction between natural and supernatural means of help which we make in cases of broken legs must also be made in cases of emotional disturbances."[1] Sanctity is no guarantee of mental health, for holiness of soul and mental health are not the same thing.

[1] Karl Stern, "Psychiatry and Faith", *Catholic Digest*, November 1955, pp. 85 ff.

Again, there are a number of psychiatrists who have no interest in, or may be actively hostile to, religion. Some are quite intolerant and contemptuous. Pierre Janet was once heard to remark that scientific psychiatry could carry on efficiently that very "cure of souls" which religion has always carried on in a bungling way.

It is therefore right and proper that co-operation between the priest and the psychiatrist should always rest upon personal knowledge and friendship, with mutual respect, and each being aware of his own limitations. There must be the firm conviction that it is to the *whole* man that both are called to minister. Co-operation cannot take place on a basis of a neat division of labour, for this only reintroduces the old dichotomy between religion and science. A clear-cut separation of the tasks of the priest and the psychiatrist can only be based on the old subdivision of spiritual versus material, in which the one has no connection or dependence upon the other. A narrowly conceived science can never work in conjunction with a narrowly conceived religion! There must be a sizeable group on either side who are willing to work with the other, if a substantial degree of collaboration is to be achieved.

COMMON PROBLEMS

The subject of guilt may serve as an example of common problems. Unfortunately, there has been much misunderstanding about this subject of guilt, yet this misunderstanding disappears when we address ourselves to a fundamental distinction. It has already been noted that real guilt and the genuine feeling of guilt that accompanies it must be distinguished from irrational or morbid feelings of guilt.

Guilt is something objective—the result of having transgressed the divine law, and a normal person is perfectly conscious of his sin. This is a genuine sense of guilt. Now only contrition, confession, and a firm purpose of amendment can take away objective guilt. Only then can a normal person cease also to feel guilty, even though he still may feel remorse for his sins, he feels happy for being free from guilt. This is beautifully expressed by the great penitent David in Psalm 32, which might be termed "Psalm Psychotherapeutic". A transposition of the verses makes the sequence of the penitent's experience clearer:

When I kept silence, my bones waxed old through my roaring all the day long.
For day and night thy hand was heavy upon me: my moisture is turned into the drought of summer.
I acknowledged my sin unto thee and mine iniquity have I not hid. I said, I will confess my transgressions unto the Lord; And thou forgavest the iniquity of my sin. . . .
Blessed is he whose transgression is forgiven, whose sin is covered. Blessed is the man unto whom the Lord imputeth not iniquity. . . .

But there is also a morbid, irrational, neurotic feeling of guilt. In some people the feeling of anxiety may continue after the sin is forgiven, it may even exist without any apparent guilt. In such cases, the individual can no longer be regarded as a penitent, but must be considered a patient who should be treated by psychiatry.

The problem becomes aggravated and disturbing when guilt becomes, not a wrong to be righted, but always a symptom of a pathological state miraculously dispersed by the "mental message" of the psychiatrist. In his *Discourse to the Delegates of the Fifth Congress of Psychotherapy and Clinical Psychology* (13 April 1953) His Holiness Pope Pius XII stated that "it is certain that no purely psychological treatment will cure a genuine sense of guilt. Even if psychotherapists, perhaps even in good faith, question its existence, it still abides. . . . As every Christian knows, the means of eliminating the fault consists in contrition and sacramental absolution by the priest. Here, it is the root of the evil, it is the fault itself, which is extirpated, even though remorse may continue to make itself felt. Nowadays, in certain pathological cases, it is not rare for the priest to send his penitent to a doctor. In the present case, the doctor should rather direct his patient toward God, and to those who have the power to remit the fault itself in the name of God."

Difficulties arise, too, when the *priest becomes suspicious of the psychiatrist*, fearing that his parishioner may be encouraged to substitute faith in the psychiatrist for a faith in God. If the psychiatrist has no Christian principles he may make light of religious experiences. Although the psychiatrist has to exercise impartiality to the best of his ability, his essential philosophy is so often conveyed, either directly or indirectly, to the patient. This realization of the conscious and the unconscious transference naturally disturbs the priest. If the psychiatrist has a completely materialistic outlook on life, the priest is rightly concerned lest the religious faith of his parishioner be disturbed.

So often again *the psychiatrist is suspicious of the priest*. Not all priests are adequately experienced to deal with the individual and his problems, and the psychiatrist fears the priest will superimpose upon the patient certain rigid theological views, which might be harmful to the emotional state. Simply to tell an anxious parishioner, at the wrong time, that all he needs is to "have faith" is just as useless, unkind, and indeed, harmful, as to tell him to pull himself together as "it's only nerves"! The priest can be of immense help in preventive care if only he realizes that his responsibilities lie not in analysing the illness, but in referring the parishioner through his local doctor to a competent psychiatrist. Under no circumstances must the priest attempt to imitate the psychiatrist. The psychiatrist is rightly as suspicious of the priest donning the "white coat" as the priest is of the psychiatrist being cloaked in the "black coat" (or purple stole!).

THE ESSENTIALS OF CO-OPERATION

The first and foremost need in co-operation seems to be better *communication*. The differences between religion and psychiatry are very real, and therefore it is essential that we have clarification and not devaluation. There is a dividing line between the domains of Religion and Psychiatry. Religion is concerned with the relationship of man to God and the supernatural sphere; whereas psychiatry deals with the relationship of man to himself and his fellow beings. Whenever we talk about psychiatry we refer to relationships, and whenever there is human relationship there is an I and Thou —two people equally important to each other and to the relationship. Religion brings into the picture a more important relationship, the relationship of man to a supermundane being—God. While the spiritual life is concerned with the upward movement of man, psychiatry deals with his downward movement into emotional and instinctual life.

However, the dividing line is not an "iron curtain" for the spheres often overlap. The priest instructs and develops man in the sphere of morals, which, of course, include his behaviour to his neighbours and to modern society; the psychiatrist leads to a deeper understanding of man's nature which, in turn, helps the individual towards a wider and fuller response to the working of religion. It is essential to try to understand each other's "language", for here misunderstandings and misinterpretations arise. Outlining the difficulties which arise in this respect, Jung stated that one of the main difficulties arose from the fact that both (priest and psychotherapist) appear to use the same language, but that this language calls up in their minds two totally different fields of association. Both can apparently use the same concept, and then are bound to acknowledge, to their amazement, that they are speaking of two different things!

To quote just one example of this, one may take the word "integration", which is the goal of all psychotherapy. It is generally agreed among psychiatrists that integration is one of the primary components of the mentally healthy personality. It is conceived as the individual's ability to create some form of unity and direction out of his own divergent impulses and aspirations. According to psychiatric thought, his ability depends to a very great extent upon the experiences in the early life of the individual and his relationship to family, parents, and environment. On the other hand, the priest, while emphasizing the need of good personal relationships, would conceive of integration being best achieved through the individual's recognition and acceptance of his relationship to God.

So often similar words are used with different meanings, and different words are used with similar meanings. On the latter point, Gordon Allport[1] made some interesting comments when he stated that "the religious vocabulary seems dignified and archaic; our scientific vocabulary, persuasive and barbaric. 'His Id and super-ego have not learned to co-operate', writes the modern mental hygienist. 'The flesh lusteth against the Spirit, and the Spirit against the flesh', writes St Paul. 'Feelings of guilt suggest poor personality team-work', says the twentieth-century specialist. 'Purify your hearts, ye double-minded', exhorts St James! 'The capacity of the ego to ward off anxiety is enlarged if the ego has considerable affection for his fellows and a positive goal to help them'. Correspondingly, St John writes, 'Perfect love casteth out fear'. It would be difficult", confessed Allport, "to find any proposition in modern mental hygiene that has not been expressed with venerable symbols in some portion of the world's religious literature."[2]

The second need is for a *well-trained priesthood*. The

[1] Gordon W. Allport, *The Individual and his Religion* (Constable 1951), p. 96.

[2] "Wilt thou be made whole?" "Physician, heal thyself", "Neither do I condemn thee", can all find their counterpart in modern psychiatric literature. So can some of the passages of the *Confessions of St Augustine*, and many a line of Francis Thompson's *Hound of Heaven*. What psychiatric text book could provide a more apt description of compulsive behaviour than Rom. 7. 18, 19: "For the good that I would I do not, but the evil that I would not, that I do. Now when I do that I would not, it is no more I that do it, but sin that dwelleth in me. I find then a law, that, when I would do good, evil is present with me. For I delight in the law of God after the inward man; But I see another law in my members, warring against the law of my mind, and bringing me into captivity to the law of sin which is in my members."

priest should be well informed about the milder symptoms of mental illness, their diagnosis, and their therapy, "not to exercise the art of mental healing, but for two reasons; partly to be able to recognize mental illness when they see it and refer the sufferer to a physician, and partly to be able to impart knowledge of the Gospel more effectively, especially to the mentally sick person who may have difficulty in understanding what Christianity is".[1]

It cannot be too greatly emphasized, however, that he behave as a well-informed priest and not as an half-informed psychiatrist! Fortunately there are now more and more opportunities available for clergy to gain greater understanding and deeper insight into the varied problems relating to mental illness and emotional disorders.[2] Conferences, meetings, and discussion groups are being arranged in which members of the different professions in the whole field of mental health come together to share common problems and mutual concerns. Interdisciplinary groups study how best they can work together and seek to clarify their own roles within the therapeutic team. A number of clergy are being involved in training in psychiatric hospitals where in the clinical environment an integrated programme of both theory and practice is held under personal supervision. Other seminars are arranged on a diocesan level to which both clergy and ministers can bring clinical material for open discussion and be given help and guidance by those who are experienced in pastoral care. In this way much goodwill is being built up between the caring professions.

The priest will then know when the spiritual approach becomes most helpful. Miss Graham Ikin suggests that: "If sufficient training in psychopathology could be given to

---

[1] Bergsten, *Pastoral Psychology*, p. 36.

[2] For information relating to the various organizations the reader is referred to *Pastoral Care and the Training of Ministers* (The British Council of Churches, 10 Eaton Gate, S.W.1, 1969) which contains a directory of the many courses and programmes being held in different centres throughout the country.

clergy to enable them to distinguish the kind of case in which their religious approach may be definitely harmful, where a faulty religious attitude would distort or nullify their efforts, their positive element in their ministry would be far more effective. Co-operation between clergy so trained and psychotherapists or psychiatrists, each passing on cases suitable to the ministry of the other would be valuable."[1]

With a background of thorough training in dealing with the emotionally disturbed, the priest's patience "will thus be strengthened by technical competence, and he will listen peacefully to the unravelling of an anguished and confused conscience. To the delicate patience of his Master when he spoke to the Samaritan woman, the priest will add the intelligent insight, full of kindness but exempt from weakness, with which Christ decided between the woman taken in adultery and her Pharisee judges."[2]

HOW THE PSYCHIATRIST CAN HELP THE PRIEST

1.   By providing new understanding concerning human behaviour. The unconscious is the most important concept in psychiatry. It has been likened to a repository in which we deposit pleasant and unpleasant experiences. In normal life they remain undisturbed, but when associated with an unusual force of emotion they are apt to upset the balance of the mind. It therefore becomes difficult sometimes to determine when our behaviour is purely the result of conscious decisions, or determined by deep, inner psychic motivations of which we are unaware.

2.   By helping the priest re-learn methods which have always belonged to the cure of souls, but have become forgotten and neglected. For example, the art of listening—one of the finest qualifications of a good priest is to know how to listen, and listen intelligently. We have been trained to be talkers, and

[1] Op. cit., pp. 86 f.
[2] Andre Snoeck, *Mental Hygiene and Christian Principles* (Mercier Press 1954), p. 44.

are therefore more prone to moralize, give out "pious platitudes", or "sermonettes".

Another lost art is concern for the individual, and respect for his unique integrity. The psychiatrist's concern starts with the individual, and the individual as he is. He helps the patient confront his past failures, deal with his present inadequacies, and to plan realistically for his future.

3. By giving to religion fresh insights into the law of individual and social health. "More and more priests have come to realize that theological doctrines must be broken open, enriched and modified in the light of modern psychology if they are to serve their own purposes most effectively . . .[many priests are] just waking up to the fact that contemporary psychotherapy along with perennial Christian resources may revitalize the healing function of the Church, and throw fresh light upon traditional doctrines."[1]

The third need is for the psychiatrist to acquaint himself with an *understanding of religion*. To learn more about the the religious aspects of his patient's beliefs and attitudes, and where they arise. At present, the traffic appears to be a little one-sided. Psychiatrists lecture to priests, visit theological colleges to address students, and participate in group discussions and seminars, but very little is said or written about the role of religion in psychiatric education.

Many psychiatrists are becoming more and more aware of the value of religion, and the need seems urgent that they be taught something of the function of religion in illness and health. Some psychiatrists are apt to confuse real religion with the pseudo-religion of many psychotic patients who use religion as a crutch in their psychological make-up. Fosdick once remarked that what many a psychologist called religion, the New Testament and the eighth-century prophets called sin; and Allport has stated that psychologists write with the frankness of Freud or Kinsey on the sexual passions of man-

---

[1] *The Church and Mental Health*, Ed. Paul Maves. Art. "Health from the standpoint of the Christian faith", David E. Roberts.

kind but blush with shame when the religious passions are brought into focus.

It must, however, be confessed that not all religious influences are favourable to sound mental health principles, and that "wrong" religion can often be as harmful as the wrong type of drug.[1] (See previous chapter.)

Yellowlees is wise to point out that "religion which is a matter of blind obedience to an authoritative list of negative commands, of things you mustn't do, through fear of punishment or hope of reward in this life or the next, is bound to breed repression and resentment and conflict, and cannot be mentally healthy. I always have a feeling of peculiar therapeutic helplessness when I am faced with a not uncommon type of neurotic patient, whose intensely narrow and rigid religious ideas are inextricably entangled with his neurotic symptoms."[2]

It is sometimes remarked that preoccupation with religion engenders mental disorder. Those in schizophrenic or depressive conditions, who suffer from theopathic delusions and utter religious formulae are held up as examples of too much religion. Preoccupation with religion is seen as an obstacle rather than a help. But, as Allport suggests, a contrary hypothesis seems equally reasonable. When people feel strange and out of touch with environment they cast around desperately for explanation of their peculiar feelings. It may be that preoccupation with religion was not the *cause* but the *effect* of the breakdown. What language, asks Allport, other than religion, can represent to disturbed patients the mysterious forces that they feel? "When imagination and emotion run wild, the symbols of religion seem most nearly adequate to the task of rationalization that faces any patient suffering from catastrophic change in personality."[3]

[1] See Wayne Oates, *Religious Factors in Mental Illness.*
[2] David Yellowlees, *Religion and Mental Health.* Lecture given at the Annual General Meeting of the Scottish Association for Mental Health, Edinburgh, 17 June 1955.
[3] Allport, op. cit.

12

As it is essential for the priest to recognize the role of psychiatry, so it should be equally essential for the psychiatrist to understand and appreciate the role that religion can play in the life of the individual. Whether the religious beliefs of the patient are viewed as symptoms or not, they should be treated with reasonable respect.

It may be true to say that in the field of the psychoses and in certain emotional difficulties, the psychiatrist can carry on his work effectively without bordering on religion, but when he is faced with problems of personality, character, the meaning and purpose of life, he can only understand such questions within a framework of values derived from a religious belief. "If psychological treatment does not issue in the change of a man's mentality, his outlook, his manner of conduct, his attitude to the world, and his place in the world", explains Victor White, "it surely fails entirely in its own set purpose. And, however we may choose to define ethics, or for that matter religion, surely we must agree that they are both concerned with these very things. It is therefore hard to see how we can agree with such a distinction between mental and spiritual or moral disorder as is sometimes suggested, or how a responsible and conscientious psychotherapist can disclaim any concern with his patient's religion and morals, and treat these as an untouchable sphere which is no concern of his."[1]

A lecture given by Alphonse Maeder on *Reflections on the Hardship and Inner Stability of the Psychiatrist* outlines the great help the Christian religion can be to a psychiatrist, continually surrounded as he is by people in anxiety and distress.

At times [he records] what he hears is so horrible that he is shaken by sympathy, disgust, or alarm. There is something intrinsically shattering in hearing certain life-stories. . . . The psychotherapist should sympathetically relive these experiences with the patient, but it is necessary at the same time to absorb the shock, to be alert, to be a support, to recognize and point out signposts. . . . Who possesses these qualities as a natural

[1] Victor White, o.p., *Soul and Psyche* (Collins & Harwill, London 1960), p. 31.

gift?... The times demand that one be strong and inwardly unified. Without the certainty and support of faith I cannot carry on. I learn over and over again that what is necessary is granted if I sincerely request it and faithfully follow His guidance. [He continues]: I know through experience that science and religion can be combined in private life whereas in my youth they seemed to be an irreconcilable contradiction.... In the Bible I find the consolation, the stimulating and direction-giving source of strength I had long sought. The Gospels and Psalms, the Epistles and the Prophets offer an inexhaustible fountain of living waters. The attentive reading and meditating of such a "message" (a kind of spiritual "mastication") provides one with new inner experiences not vouchsafed to the purely intellectually-orientated person. Without a knowledge of man's religious life, psychiatry surely becomes an incomplete act.

HOW THE PRIEST CAN HELP THE PSYCHIATRIST IN RETURN

1. By teaching the right type of religion, which is of immense value to true peace of soul. In this way, the priest contributes to the mental health of his people. Once a person realizes he is created in the image of God, he finds personal value and dignity. Once he realizes God's providence he can so often escape the threat of fear and anxiety.

2. By the use of the sacraments. The priest is the only person who, by nature of his divine calling, can accept repentance and forgive sins. For the Christian, guilt is centred in the I and Thou relationship between God and himself. It is in the divine forgiveness of sins that the priest has a function and duty to perform that goes far beyond what is possible to the psychiatrist. In the sacrament of Penance, the priest deals with a great force, which is why the friendly psychiatrist looks at him with hope and encouragement, and the unfriendly one with alarm and dismay.

3. By giving something which is really positive and satisfying to replace faulty patterns of behaviour. Psychiatry is essentially an analysing process. Religion is a synthesizing process. In the foreword to Victor White's, *God and the*

Unconscious, Jung himself reminds us that "neurosis is no isolated, sharp to define phenomenon, it is a reaction of the whole human being... modern medicine has just begun to take account of this fact... long years of experience have again and again taught me that a therapy along purely biological lines does not suffice, but requires a spiritual completion".

Not only must the mind be swept, but no room must be left for the seven other spirits more wicked than the first, for if these enter and dwell there "the last state of that man is worse than the first" (Matt. 12. 44; Luke 11. 25).

4. By presenting the "utterly reliable love of God", for we are told that much conflict of mind is caused by the lack of security, a fear of being unloved. According to Dr Denis Martin, "much illness would be relieved or even cured, if people really fully accepted that God loves them just as they are and not only when they are good, or even when they strive to live up to some expected Christian ethic. Emotional acceptance of this truth is essential if it is to be effective. The individual needs a 'feeling experience' of the reality of God's love. The neurotic suffers above all others from the fear of 'Thou shalt not', and instinctively reasons 'if I do, I shall not be loved'."[1] "Perfect love casteth out fear" becomes as vital a truth for good psychiatry as it is for religion.

5. By realizing the limitations of his abilities, and being most careful not to overstep them. He should know when the doctor or psychiatrist is to be called in. When the problems with which he deals become protracted and prolonged, when they are beyond his understanding, and the scope of his time, he must realize that the stage is being reached for competent psychiatric attention.

Between *real* psychiatry and *true* religion there can be no fundamental incompatibility. The nature of man, the pur-

[1] Denis Martin, "Religion and Healing" in *Mental Health*, Vol. XVII, No. 3.

pose of his existence, and the fulfilment of his destiny are fundamental concepts in both professions, and where the integrity and worth of the individual soul is respected, there can be no conflict. It is in the varying approaches to these factors that apparent discord lies for both the theologian and the psychiatrist are concerned with human nature and human behaviour. Where there is a radical difference of philosophy in these two realms, it is not strange that conflicts and misunderstandings arise.

As priest and psychiatrist work together towards active co-operation it should not surprise both parties to discover not merely additional opportunities for mutual help, but also conflicts of which both are not presently aware. If these occur in the sphere of co-operation and goodwill they are most welcome and appreciated, for they will lead to a more secure co-operation and a greater understanding. If they go forward with courage and humility on both sides, the priest and the psychiatrist can then hope to clear many misunderstandings of the past, break down many obstacles of the present, and enlarge many areas for the future.

Bibliography

CHAPTER 1

GENERAL READING

Psychiatry Today, by D. Stafford-Clark (Penguin)

New Horizons in Psychiatry, by P. Hays (Penguin)

Adventure in Psychiatry, by D. Martin (Cassirer)

The Church: a Healing Community, by D. Martin (Guild of Health)

Psychiatric Hospital Care, by H. J. Freeman (Bailliere, Tindall and Cassell)

Living with Mental Illness, by E. Mills (Routledge and Kegan Paul)

To Tell the Truth: Mental Hospitals Today, by N. Roberts (N.A.M.H.)

Mental Health and Mental Illness, by N. Roberts (Routledge and Kegan Paul)

Community, Church, and Healing, by R. A. Lambourne (Darton, Longman and Todd)

The Caring Church, ed. by P. Smith (Peter Smith)

An Approach to Community Mental Health, by G. Caplan (Tavistock Publications)

Home Care for the Emotionally Ill, by H. S. Schwartz (Staples Press)

PROBLEMS OF CHILDHOOD

Child Care and the Growth of Love, by J. Bowlby (Penguin)

The Child and the Family, by D. W. Winnicott (Tavistock Publications)

The Child, the Family, and the Outside World, by D. W. Winnicott (Penguin)

The Normal Child and Some of His Abnormalities, by C. W. Valentine (Penguin)

PROBLEMS OF ADOLESCENCE

The Unattached, by N. Morse (Penguin)
Journey through Adolescence, by D. Odlum (Penguin)
Teenagers Today, by G. S. Prince (N.A.M.H.)
Teenage Tensions, in *Mental Health,* Spring 1967
Teenagers and Drugs (Councils and Education Press, London)

PROBLEMS OF MIDDLE-AGE

Men in Middle Life, by K. Saddy with M. C. Kidson (Tavistock Pub.)
The Middle-aged Man, by A. Torrie (C.I.O.)
The Noon-day Devil, by B. Bassett (Burns Oates)
Change of Life, by J. Malleson (Penguin)

PROBLEMS OF OLD AGE

On Growing Old, by S. Harton (Hodder)
The Process of Ageing, by A. Comfort (Bayliss)
The Psychology of Human Ageing, by D. B. Bromley (Penguin)
Understanding Old Age, by R. Emery (N.A.M.H.)

CHAPTER 2

The Casework Relationship, by F. Biestek (S.C.M. Press)
Games People Play, by E. Berne (Penguin)
Principles of Pastoral Counselling, by R. S. Lee (S.P.C.K. Library of Pastoral Care)
The Faith of the Counsellors, by P. Halmos (Constable)
The Pastor as Counsellor, by A. Godin (Logos Books, Mercier Press)
Pastoral Counselling, by S. Hiltner (Abingdon-Cokesbury)
The Meaning of Persons, by P. Tournier (S.C.M. Press)
An Introduction of Teaching Casework Skills, by J. Heywood (Routledge and Kegan Paul)
Pastoral Counselling: Its Theory and Practise, by C. A. Wise (Harper: Hamilton)
Counselling and Psychotherapy, by C. Rogers (Houghton Mifflin)
I and Thou, by M. Buber (T. and T. Clark)
Counselling and Social Welfare, by J. H. Wallis (Routledge and Kegan Paul)

CHAPTER 3

Psychosomatic Medicine: Its Principles and Application, by F. Alexander (Allen and Unwin)
Body and Soul, by P. Dearmer (Pitman)
Mind and Body: Psychosomatic Medicine, by F. Dunbar (Vision and Mayflower)
Psychosomatics, by M. Hamilton (Chapman and Hall)
Health, Disease, and Integration, by H. P. Newsholme (Allen and Unwin)
A Psychosomatic Approach to Medicine, by D. O'Neill (Pitman Medical)
The Body: A Study in Pauline Theology, by J. A. T. Robinson (S.C.M. Press)
The Stress of Life, by H. Selye (Longmans)
The Psychosomatic Disorders (Mental Health Research Fund)

FOR REFERENCE

Psychosomatic Medicine, by E. Weiss and O. S. English (W. B. Saunders)
Recent Developments in Psychosomatic Medicine, by E. D. Wittkower and R. A. Cleghorn (Pitman Medical)

CHAPTERS 4 and 5

GENERAL

What Freud Really Said, by D. Stafford-Clark (Penguin)
Mental Illness and Social Work, by E. Heimler (Penguin)
The Psychotic, by A. Crowcroft (Penguin)
Psychiatry in the Modern World, by E. B. Strauss (Michael Joseph)
Clinical Psychiatry for Practitioners and Students, by I. Skittowe (Eyre)
Anxiety, Nervousness, and Depression, by F. R. C. Casson (B.M.A.)
The Integrity of the Personality, by A. Storr (Penguin)
Freud and the Post-Freudians, by J. A. C. Brown (Penguin)
Psychiatry Today, by D. Stafford-Clark (Penguin)
Freud and Christianity, by R. S. Lee (Penguin)

Psychiatry for Students, by D. Stafford-Clark (Allen and Unwin)
Healing the Sick Mind, by H. Guntrip (Allen and Unwin)
The Divided Self, by R. D. Laing (Penguin)

MENTAL SUBNORMALITY

All Children are Special, Report (C.I.O.)
Children at Risk, Report (C.I.O.)
Number Unknown, Report (C.I.O.)
Mental Subnormality, by A. Heaton-Ward (Stonebridge Press)
Play Activities for the Retarded Child, by B. W. Carlson and D. R. Ginglend (Cassell)
Subnormal Personalities, by C. J. C. Earl (Balliere, Tindall and Cassell)
Teaching the Severely Subnormal, Ed. E. B. MacDowall (Edward Arnold Ltd)
Mentally Handicapped and Their Families, by J. Tizard and J. C. Grad (Oxford University Press)
Mental Deficiency, by R. F. Tredgold and K. Soddy (Balliere, Tindall, and Cassell)
Autistic Children, by L. Wing (N.A.M.H.)
The Mentally Retarded Child, by A. Levinson (Allen and Unwin)
The Hand of the Potter, by N. & P. Motte (Cassell)

ALCOHOLISM

Understanding and Counselling the Alcoholic, by H. J. Clinebell (Abingdon Press)
How to Help an Alcoholic, by C. Earle (Westminster Press)
Primer on Alcoholism, by M. Mann (Victor Gollancz)
Alcoholism, its Psychology and Cure, by F. B. Rea (Epworth Press)
Alcoholism: Manual for Students and Practitioners, by L. Williams (Livingstone)
Tomorrow will be Sober, by L. Williams (Cassell)
The Alcoholic and the Family (The Church of England Temperance Society)

The Christian Approach to the Alcoholic, by J. B. Harrison (Reprint from *The Friend*)

Alcoholic Addiction: A Psycho-social Approach to Abnormal Drinking, by H. Jones (Tavistock)

Depth Psychology, Morality, and Alcoholism, by J. C. Ford (Burns Oates)

The Origin of Alcoholism, by W. and J. McCord (Tavistock)

Alcoholism, N. Kessel and H. Walton (Penguin)

DRUG DEPENDENCE

Drug Dependence in Britain, Information Paper (C.I.O.)

Alcohol and Drugs (S.P.C.K. Hidden Dangers Series)

Addiction—Drugs and Alcohol (*Mental Health*, Autumn 1966)

Drugs and Young People, by Sister Superior, Spelthorne St. Mary (Mothers Union)

Drug Dependence, by A. J. Wood (Health Dept., Tower Hill, Bristol 2)

Aspects of Drug Addiction, by M. Silverman (Royal London Prisoners' Aid Society)

The Addict in the Street, by J. Larner and R. Tefferteller (Penguin)

Turn Me On, Man, by A. Bestic (Tandem)

Drugs, by P. Laurie (Penguin)

Drugs for Young People—Their Use and Abuse, by C. Leech and B. Jordan

Drug Dependence, by J. H. Willis (Faber and Faber)

L.S.D., Man and Society, Ed. by R. C. De Bold (Faber and Faber)

SUICIDE

Suicide and Attempted Suicide, by E. Stengel (Penguin)

The Samaritans, by C. Varah (Constable)

Suicide, Why Not? (S.P.C.K. Pamphlets)

The Cry for Help, by N. L. Farberow and E. S. Shneidman (McGraw-Hill)

Suicide, by K. Durkheim (Routledge and Kegan Paul)

Man Against Himself, by K. Menninger (Harcourt)

Suicide in London, by P. Sainsbury (Chapman and Hall)

Prevention of Suicide, W.H.O. Public Health Paper No. 35

PASTORAL CARE

The Courage to Be, by P. Tillich (Nesbit)

The Priest and Mental Health, edited by E. F. O'Doherty and S. D. McGrath (Burns Oates)

Psychiatry and the Christian, by J. Dominian (Faith and Fact Book, Burns Oates)

The Role of Religion in Mental Health, Report (N.A.M.H.)

The Church and Mental Health, edited by P. Maves (Scribners)

A Christian Therapy for a Neurotic World, by E. N. Ducker (Allen and Unwin)

Religious Factors in Mental Illness, by W. Oates (Allen and Unwin)

Clinical Theology, by F. Lake (Darton, Longman and Todd)

Mental First-Aid, by N. Small (S.P.C.K.)

The Priest and the Sick in Mind, by A. A. A. Terruwe (Burns Oates)

Pastoral Care in Hospitals, by N. Autton (S.P.C.K. Library of Pastoral Care)

The Priest and the Unconscious, by E. Ringel and W. Van Lun (Mercier Press)

CHAPTER 6

Anxiety and Neurosis, by C. Rycroft (Penguin)

Textbook of Psychiatry, by D. K. Henderson and R. D. Gillespie (Oxford Medical)

Clinical Psychiatry, by W. Mayer-Gross, E. Slater and M. Roth (Cassell)

Introduction to Physical Methods of Treatment in Psychiatry by W. Sargant and E. Slater (Livingstone)

Psychiatry for Students, by D. Stafford-Clark (Allen and Unwin)

Social Psychiatry, by M. Jones (Tavistock)

Clinical Psychiatry for Practitioners and Students, by I. Skottowe (Eyre)

The Integrity of the Personality, by A. Storr (Heinemann)

The Ethics of Brain Surgery, edited by Dom P. Flood (Mercier Press)

You and Psychiatry, by W. Menninger (Scribners)

The Divided Self, by R. D. Laing (Penguin)

Group Psychotherapy, by S. H. Foulkes and E. J. Anthony (Penguin)

CHAPTER 7

Holiness is Wholeness, by J. Goldbrunner (Burns Oates)

Nervous Disorders and Religion, by J. G. McKenzie (Allen and Unwin)

Anxiety in Christian Experience, by W. Oates (Allen and Unwin)

God and the Unconscious, by V. White (Collins)

Soul and Psyche, by V. White (Collins)

The Exploration of the Inner World, by A. Boisen (Harper)

Pastoral Psychology, by G. Bergsten (Allen and Unwin)

Conflict and Light, by Père Bruno de Jesus-Marie (Sheed and Ward)

Psychology, Religion, and Human Need, by W. L. Carrington (Epworth Press)

The Church's Ministry of Healing, by A. H. P. Fox (Longmans)

Psychology and Morals, by J. A. Hadfield (Allen and Unwin)

Psychology, Religion and Healing, by L. Weatherhead (Hodder and Stoughton)

CHAPTER 8

Integration of Religion and Psychiatry, by E. W. Biddle (Macmillan, N.Y.)

Pastoral Care and the Training of Ministers, Report (B.C.C.)

Clinical Theology, by F. Lake (Darton, Longman and Todd)

Psychotherapy and the Christian View of Man, by D. Roberts (Scribners)

The Third Revolution, by K. Stern (Michael Joseph)

The Role of Religion in Mental Health, Report (N.A.M.H.)

The Individual and His Religion, by G. Allport (Constable)

Psychiatry and the Christian, by J. Dominian (Burns Oates)

The Self in Pilgrimage, by E. Loomis (S.C.M. Press)

Guilt and Grace, by P. Tournier (Hodder and Stoughton)

Mental Hygiene and Christian Principles, by A. Snoeck (Mercier Press)

Anxiety and Faith, by C. Stinnette (Seabury Press)

Soundings (Essay 4), Edited by A. Vidler (Cambridge University Press)

A Glossary of Psychiatric Concepts and Terms useful for Priests

ABREACTION

An emotional release that results from recalling to awareness a painful experience, which has been repressed because it was intolerable to conscious awareness. This release or discharge is often induced by drugs. The therapeutic effect is through discharge of painful emotions.

ACROPHOBIA

Morbid fear of heights.

ADDICTION

A strong emotional dependence upon alcohol or drug, which has progressed beyond voluntary control.

ADJUSTMENT

The relative state of harmony of the personality. Relation between the individual, his inner self, and his environment.

ADLER: ALFRED (1870–1939)

The distinguished Austrian psychiatrist, who proposed a concept of psychiatric theory known as Individual Psychology.

AFFECT

The emotional feeling-tone of a person.

AFFECTIVE PSYCHOSIS

A psychotic reaction in which there is a severe disorder of mood, or emotional feelings.

AGORAPHOBIA

Morbid fear of open spaces.

ALCOHOLISM

Habitual intake of alcohol, so that one's physical and/or mental health are seriously affected.

AMBIVALENCE

Mixed feelings, usually the simultaneous presence of opposite emotional feelings (love and hate toward the same person).

AMENTIA

Defective mental functioning. The condition is usually organic and due to a lack of adequate brain tissue.

AMNESIA

Loss of memory, either total or partial.

ANALYSAND

The patient in psycho-analytical treatment.

ANALYSIS

An intensive psychotherapeutic approach.

ANIMA

The unconscious or inner feminine potentialities in men, as formulated in Jungian psychology.

ANIMUS

The unconscious or inner male potentialities in women, as formulated in Jungian psychology.

ANOREXIA NERVOSA

Condition marked by absence of appetite, accompanying weight loss, and other nervous symptoms on an emotional basis.

ANTHROPOPHOBIA

Morbid fear of people.

ANXIETY

Tension or uneasiness, stemming from the imminent anticipation of danger, when the source is largely unknown or unrecognized. Fear in the absence of an apparently adequate cause.

APATHY

State of reactive absence of emotions, want of feeling, or lack of emotion.

APHASIA

Loss of ability to pronounce words, or to name correctly common objects or to indicate their use.

AQUAPHOBIA

Morbid fear of water.

ASSOCIATION

A relationship between ideas or emotions.

AURA

A premonitory wave of subjective sensation usually preceding an epileptic seizure.

AUTOMATISM

Mechanical symbolic behaviour outside of conscious control. Often seen in schizophrenia.

BEHAVIOURISM

A school of psychology concerned exclusively with tangible, measurable phenomena. Excludes consideration of anything subjective (Ideas, feelings, etc.).

BIRTH TRAUMA

The psychic shock of birth.

BLOCKING

The inability to recall, or the interruption of thought or speech, due to emotional factors usually out of conscious awareness.

BRAIN-WASHING

The emotional and mental processing or conditioning of prisoners, aimed at securing attitudes which conform to the wishes of the captors.

CATATONIA

A clinical type of schizophrenia characterized by immobility with muscle rigidity.

CATHARSIS

The release of ideas through "talking out" of conscious material. Considerable relief and loss of tension usually follows.

CENSOR

A term used by Freud which envisages a part of the unconscious self-functioning as a guardian to prevent the emergence into consciousness of repressed material.

CENTRAL NERVOUS SYSTEM

The brain and spinal cord.

CEREBELLUM

The lower back part of the brain, having to do largely with co-ordination.

CLAUSTROPHOBIA

Morbid fear of closed spaces.

CLIMACTERIC

Menopause.

COLLECTIVE UNCONSCIOUS

A term used by Jung for that portion of the unconscious which is theoretically common to mankind.

COMA

A state of complete loss of consciousness in which there is no perception or voluntary movement possible.

COMPENSATION

A mental mechanism outside and beyond conscious awareness by which the individual attempts to make up for real or fancied deficiencies.

COMPLEX

A group of associated ideas which have a common strong emotional tone.

CONATIVE

Pertaining to the basic strivings of an individual, as expressed in his behaviour and actions.

CONDITIONED REFLEX

An induced reflex developed by training in association with a particular stimulus. Pavlov's theory and illustrated by a dog given food at the same time as a bell is rung. After period of conditioning the ringing of the bell alone will bring saliva and the same responses originally present when food alone was presented.

CONSCIOUSNESS

The state of awareness of one's internal and external environment.

CONSTITUTIONAL TYPES

The best known are those proposed by Kretschmer: pyknic, melancholic, athletic, and dysplastic types.

CONVERSION

Psychiatric term denoting a symbolic manifestation of an emotional conflict through motor or sensory symptoms (weakness, numbness).

CORTEX

The outer layer of the brain; cerebral cortex.

COUNTERTRANSFERENCE

The emotional reaction of the therapist to his patient.

DELIRIUM TREMENS

An acute delirium occurring in severe chronic alcoholism upon withdrawal of alcohol.

DELUSION

A false belief which is not shaken by argument, or even by demonstration of its falsity.

DEMENTIA

Generally used to refer to the advanced chronic cases of psychotic illness.

DEMENTIA PRAECOX

An older descriptive term for schizophrenia.

DEPRESSION

An extended emotional state characterized by deep melancholy, guilt, etc.

DEPTH PSYCHOLOGY

Systems of psychology which deal with intrapsychic phenomena, as opposed to those which are primarily concerned with more superficial, i.e. behavioural phenomena.

DIPSOMANIA

Compulsive drinking, frequently associated with behaviour disturbances.

DISORIENTATION

Loss of awareness of the position of oneself in relation to space, time, or persons.

DISSOCIATION

A psychological separation or splitting off.

DRIVE

A basic urge.

DULY AUTHORIZED OFFICER

Former title of an official of a Local Authority who, among other duties, is by statute required to take the initial steps for placing persons of unsound mind under control, and for obtaining reception orders for their detention. Now known as MENTAL WELFARE OFFICER.

DYNAMIC PSYCHIATRY

As opposed to descriptive psychiatry. Related to the study of emotional processes, their origins and mental mechanisms.

ECHOLALIA

The automatic repetition of phrases or words observed in certain schizophrenic disorders.

E.C.T.

Electro-convulsive therapy.

E.E.G.

Electro-encephalogram. A recording of minute electrical impulses arising from the activity of cells in the cerebral cortex of the brain.

EGO

The central part of the personality; the individual; the real self.

ELECTRA COMPLEX

From the Greek drama: "Electra", who induced her brother to murder their mother in revenge for the murder of Agamemnon, their father. Used to refer to the hostile feelings of a daughter towards her mother, arising out of competition for the affection of the father-husband.

EMOTION

A subjective feeling such as fear, anger, grief, etc.

EMPATHY

An objective awareness and understanding of the feelings, emotions, and behaviour of another person.

ENCEPHALITIS

Softening of the brain.

ENDOCRINE GLANDS

Important group of glands which secrete hormones which control growth and metabolism.

EUPHORIA

An exaggerated feeling of physical and emotional well-being.

EXTRAVERSION

A state in which attention and energies are largely directed outward from oneself. Interest mainly in external activities, as opposed to interest directed internally toward oneself, as in intraversion.

FANTASY

An imaginary sequence of events or mental images.

FIXATION

The arrest or cessation of personality development at some given point in the maturity process.

FREE ASSOCIATION

The unedited production of thoughts verbally and in sequence as they occur to conscious awareness. A vital necessity to psycho-analytical treatment.

FREUD, SIGMUND (1856–1939)

A Viennese psychiatrist who founded psycho-analysis and formulated many of the basic tenets of dynamic psychiatry.

FUGUE
   A major state of personality dissociation, characterized by
   loss of memory.

GESTALT PSYCHOLOGY
   A school of psychology noted for its shift away from the older
   traditional direction of attention to single elements of behaviour, to the study of larger areas and totality of function.

GUILT
   The subjective feeling of having committed error or sin. The
   amount of guilt does not necessarily correspond to the real
   amount of injury caused.

HALLUCINATION
   A perception occurring in the absence of any sensation. The
   person sees a "vision", and hears a "voice".

HETEROSEXUAL
   The normal sexual relationships between male and female.

HERD INSTINCT
   Social instinct. The supposed innate need of man to belong
   to a group or to conform to its standard.

HOMOSEXUALITY
   Sexual attraction or relationship between members of the
   same sex.

HYPOMANIA
   A moderately elated emotional state which is a mild form of
   manic-depressive psychosis.

HYPNOSIS
   A trance-like mental state produced by suggestion.

HYSTERIA
   An illness resulting from emotional conflict.

ID
   The unconscious instinctive desires and strivings of the personality.

ILLUSION
   The misinterpretation of a real, external sensory experience.
   A false perception.

IMPULSE
   A psychic striving.

INFERIORITY COMPLEX
   A condition of self-doubt, with feelings of inferiority.

INFORMAL PATIENT

A patient who voluntarily seeks admission to a psychiatric hospital.

INHIBITION

A restraint of thought, feeling, or action.

INSANITY

The legal term still currently used for serious psychological illness.

INSTINCT

An urgent, innate impulse or stimulus.

INSULIN THERAPY

Introduced by Sakel in Vienna in 1933. Treatment carried out by injection of insulin, and used in schizophrenic disorders.

INTRAVERSION

Turning one's interests inward.

INVOLUTIONAL PSYCHOSIS

A psychotic reaction taking place during the involutional period (40–55 Years), and characterized most commonly by depression.

I.Q.

Intelligence quotient.

JUNG, CARL GUSTAV (1875–1961)

Swiss psychiatrist, founder of the school of Analytic Psychology.

KLEPTOMANIA

Compulsive stealing; largely without regard to an outward and apparent personal need for the stolen object.

LIBIDO

Sexual desire and energy. Also used in broader sense to connote psychic energy, associated with instincts in general.

MANIA

A mental illness marked by heightened excitability. May alternate with depressive attacks.

MASOCHISM

Conscious or unconscious enjoyment of experiencing physical or mental pain.

MELANCHOLIA

An emotional state of utter dejection.

MENTAL SUBNORMALITY
Condition resulting from inadequate initial endowment at birth.

MENTAL HEALTH WORKER
A social worker employed by the Local Health Authority in duties relating to the care and after-care of patients suffering from mental illness. Also concerned with the welfare of the mentally subnormal.

MENTAL MECHANISM
An unconscious attempt at resolution of an emotional conflict. Among the more common mental mechanisms are—overcompensation; displacement; fantasy; idealization; introjection; projection; rationalization; sublimation.

MENTAL WELFARE OFFICER
See Duly Authorized Officer.

MESMERISM
An early term for hypnosis (after Mesmer, 1735–1815, an Austrian who used hypnosis in treatment in the early nineteenth century in Paris).

MYSOPHOBIA
A morbid fear of dirt, germs, or contamination.

NARCISSISM
Self-love.

NARCO-ANALYSIS
Psychotherapeutic techniques employed under the influence of drugs.

NARCOSIS
A sleep-like state, induced by a narcotic drug.

NERVOUS BREAKDOWN
A general, unspecific term for emotional illness.

NEUROSIS
An emotional illness or disorder without marked loss of contact with reality in thinking and judgement.

OBSESSION
An insistent, repetitive, and unwanted thought.

OCCUPATIONAL THERAPY
The patient's interests are partly stimulated and occupied in supervised, constructive handicrafts, manual pursuits, etc., and in industrial therapy.

OEDIPAL PERIOD
Stage of development from 3–6 years.

OEDIPUS COMPLEX
The emotional attachment by a boy to his mother, with hostility towards his father.

OLIGOPHOBIA
Mental subnormality.

ORAL STAGE
The first stage of the infantile period in sexual development, lasting from birth to 12 months, or even to two years.

ORGANIC PSYCHOSIS
A psychosis of organic aetiology, as distinguished from a psychosis of emotional origin.

ORGASM
The climax in sexual relations.

ORIENTATION
Awareness of oneself in relation to one's spatial, temporal, and interpersonal situations.

PARANOIA
A very slow and chronic form of schizophrenia.

PARESIS
A psychosis resulting from syphilitic infection of the brain.

PERCEPTION
Awareness.

PERSONA
In Jungian psychology, the personality "mask" or facade which each person presents to the outside world.

PERSONALITY
The sum total of the person.

PHOBIA
A pathological fear.

PLAY THERAPY
A psychotherapeutic approach to children's emotional disorders in which observation and interpretation of the child's use of his toys, clay, paints, etc., form an important part of the therapy.

PREFRONTAL LEUCOTOMY
See Psychosurgery.

PROJECTION

The attributing to another of one's own repressed, unconscious motivations.

PSYCHE

The mind.

PSYCHIATRIC SOCIAL WORKER

A social worker with a special training and qualification who works in co-operation with the psychiatrist.

PSYCHIATRIST

A physician with special post-graduate training and experience in the field of emotional illness and mental disorders.

PSYCHIATRY

A basic medical science which deals with the genesis, diagnosis, prevention, and treatment of emotional illness and mental disorders.

PSYCHO-ANALYSIS

A system of therapy, the original outlines and foundations for which were laid down by Freud. Treatment seeks to modify emotions and behaviour by bringing into awareness the origin and effect of the unconscious emotional conflicts, with increased understanding of the feelings associated with them.

PSYCHO-ANALYST

A psychiatrist with special post-graduate training who employs the techniques of psycho-analysis.

PSYCHODRAMA

A technique of group psychotherapy, developed by Moreno, in which individuals dramatize their emotional problems through playing assigned roles.

PSYCHOLOGY

The branch of science devoted to the study of mental processes and behaviour.

PSYCHOLOGY, ANALYTIC

The system of Carl Jung.

PSYCHOLOGY, INDIVIDUAL

The system of Alfred Adler.

PSYCHONEUROSIS

See Neurosis.

PSYCHOPATH

One suffering from a character neurosis of an asocial and antisocial type.

PSYCHOPATHIC PERSONALITY

One whose behaviour is impulsive, irresponsible, with unstable emotional and social adaptation.

PSYCHOPATHOLOGY

The branch of science which deals with emotional and psychological processes and their development.

PSYCHOSIS

A severe mental disorder. The sufferer has little or no insight into his condition.

PSYCHOSOMATIC

Adjective used to describe serious emotional disorders which are manifested primarily in terms of physical illness.

PSYCHOSOMATIC MEDICINE

The study of a patient as an integrated organism consisting of body, mind, and spirit.

PSYCHOSURGERY

The treatment of functional psychotic disorders by means of brain surgery.

PSYCHOTHERAPY

Name for any type of treatment based primarily upon communication with the patient in the interview, as opposed to use of drugs, physical measures, or surgery.

PUERPERAL PSYCHOSIS

A psychotic episode having its onset in the puerperal (childbirth) period.

RATIONALIZATION

The attempt to make unknown and irrational things appear reasonable and logical.

REGRESSION

The psychic process of returning to an earlier and subjectively more satisfactory (but actually more infantile) level of adjustment.

REPRESSION

The involuntary relegation of unbearable ideas and impulses from conscious awareness into the unconscious, from whence they are not ordinarily subject to voluntary conscious recall.

RESISTANCE

A patient's conscious or unconscious reluctance to relinquish established patterns of behaviour; opposition and reluctance to change.

RORSCHACH TEST

A personality assessment test developed by Rorschach (1884–1922), a Swiss psychiatrist, whereby conscious and unconscious personality traits and emotional conflicts are disclosed by the patient's responses to a standard set of ink-blots.

SADISM

The derivation of pleasure, often sexual, from inflicting pain or discomfort on another person.

SCHIZOID

Shy, withdrawn, introspective, and introverted. Schizophrenic traits and reactions.

SCHIZOPHRENIA

A group of severe emotional disorders most frequently occurring in late adolescence. Retreat from reality.

SENTIMENT

A feeling or emotional attitude.

SPLIT PERSONALITY

A lay term often employed for schizophrenia.

STATUS EPILEPTICUS

A serious state of more or less continuous epileptic seizures.

STUPOR

A state in which the individual has little or no appreciation of his surroundings.

SUBCONSCIOUS

The level of mind which is accessible to more or less voluntary recall.

SUBLIMATION

The direction of undesirable or forbidden tendencies into more socially acceptable channels.

SUGGESTIBILITY

Ready change of mind, attitude, or behaviour in accord with what another person suggests.

SUICIDE

Act of self-destruction.

SUPER-EGO

Frequently used synonymously with the conscience.

SUPPRESSION

The conscious effort to subjugate unacceptable thoughts or desires.

TEMPERAMENT

The set frame of mind or mental and emotional character of an individual.

TOXIC PSYCHOSIS

A psychosis resulting from the effect of various toxic agents.

TRAIT

A characteristic.

TRANCE

A sleep-like state in which consciousness is partially or entirely suspended.

TRANQUILLIZING DRUGS

A group of drugs used in psychosis and other conditions for their sedative and anxiety-relieving effects.

TRANSFERENCE

The unconscious attitude of the patient toward the therapist who may be thought of as standing in some parental, rivalrous, erotic, or other role.

TRAUMA

Psychological or physical injury.

UNCONSCIOUS

The forces and content of the mind which are not ordinarily available to conscious awareness or to immediate recall.

VOLITION

The act or power of making one's own free choice or decision.

Index of Persons, Organizations, etc.

General Index